1975

DAYS

Milton: The Modern Phase

Milton:
The Modern Phase

A Study of Twentieth-century Criticism

PATRICK MURRAY

NEW YORK

BARNES & NOBLE, INC.

Publishers · Booksellers · Since 1897

Published in the United States
in 1967
by Barnes & Noble, Inc.
105 Fifth Avenue, New York

Printed in Great Britain

Contents

Preface

The enormous bulk of Milton criticism and scholarship makes it rather difficult to justify a further contribution, particularly if that contribution has little or nothing to offer in the way of clarification or interpretation of particular aspects of Milton's work. This book is, however, historical rather than scholarly or critical in its method: in the chapters that follow I have tried to provide a general survey of the work of twentieth-century critics and scholars. I have also traced the course of the Milton Controversy, examined some modern objections to *Paradise Lost*, and described in general terms the vicissitudes suffered by Milton's reputation since 1900.

Several writers have dealt with the modern questioning of his major status, but mainly in passing. These chapters were written in the conviction that a brief history of modern Milton criticism was called for. By bringing together the results of other people's work I hope I have shown how Milton appears in the light of contemporary critical opinion. I have dealt exclusively with criticism of *Paradise Lost*, on which, by common consent, Milton's position in English literature depends.

I should like to thank Professor C. L. Wrenn for his advice and encouragement.

Patrick Murray

Abbreviations

The following abbreviations are used:

Bohn   J. A. St John's edition of Milton's prose works in Bohn's Universal Library (5 vols. 1848–53)

ELH   Journal of English Literary History

ESEA   Essays and Studies by Members of the English Association

JEGP   Journal of English and German Philology

MLR   Modern Language Review

PBA   Proceedings of the British Academy

PMLA   Publications of the Modern Language Association

RES   Review of English Studies

SP   Studies in Philology

TLS   *The Times Literary Supplement*

The place of publication of books cited in the references is London, unless otherwise stated.

CHAPTER ONE

The Modern Reaction

The second decade of the twentieth century marked a turning-point in the history of Milton criticism. It saw the beginning of a new attitude to Milton and his work, and the end of a critical tradition which had held its ground for over two centuries. All the major English critics from Dryden to Sir Walter Raleigh had been agreed on his position among the English poets: he was, in Coleridge's phrase, 'Shakespeare's compeer, not rival'. There had, it is true, been minor expressions of dissent, but most of these had been based on avowed hostility to Milton's political views. When Johnson ventured some unfavourable remarks on Milton and his work, his own reputation as a critic suffered, and he was the subject of abuse and even ridicule from admirers of Milton like Cowper. Johnson's contemporary Lord Chesterfield admitted in a letter to his son that he could not read Milton through; he did not however, want this known, lest he should be abused by 'every tasteless Pedant and every solid Divine in England'. Havens, who examined most of the evidence, came to the conclusion that from Pope's day to Wordsworth's, 'Milton occupied a place, not only in English literature, but in the thought and life of Englishmen of all classes, which no poet has held since, and none is likely to hold again'.[1] And from Wordsworth's day to Raleigh's, there was no marked decline in his prestige.

In the early twentieth century, the verdict which had commanded such widespread assent from poets and critics for over two hundred years was challenged. For the first time in the history of Milton criticism, a sustained attack was made on his work by influential critics. In previous centuries it had been the custom to compare him with Shakespeare. Middleton Murry's reaction to such comparisons was unfavourable: 'There is not much sense, really, in these concatenations.' Ezra Pound's reaction was more extreme and more violent. He suggested that Milton's real place was nearer to Drummond of Hawthornden than to Shakespeare or Dante, 'whereto the stupidity of our forebears tried to exalt him'. In 1930 Herbert Read could claim with some justification that the critical conception of Milton was undergoing an almost complete transformation, the process being, as he saw it, 'one of disintegration'. And F. R. Leavis was glad that by 1933 Milton's dislodgement had been effected 'with remarkably little fuss'.[2]

The modern case against Milton was first clearly stated by Ezra Pound. His passing observations, all of them hostile, anticipated the main charges brought by later critics. He censured Milton's diction and syntax, blamed him for using an uninflected language as if it were an inflected one, and expressed his disgust with 'what he has to say, his asinine bigotry, his beastly hebraism'. He had even more important reservations to express. These reservations concerned Milton's influence on the poetry of the past: they were shared by critics like Eliot and Leavis, who believed that English poetry had to be freed from Miltonic influence and allowed to develop along new lines. Poets in revolt against a decadent tradition saw in Milton its chief representative; Eliot suggested that his influence could only be bad for the young modern poet, and Pound warned neophytes that the study of Milton would set them 'trying to pile up noise and adjectives'.[3]

What was later to be called the Milton Controversy had its origin in the disparaging remarks about Milton's influence made by Pound and Eliot. The work of these critics marks a distinct phase in the history of Milton criticism, for they wrote primarily as practising poets, not as scholars or critics. For them, the really important question was: From what earlier poets can the modern poet most profitably learn? Eliot pointed out that his criticism was a by-product of his own 'private poetry workshop', a prolongation of the thinking that went into the production of his poetry. And Pound, Eliot explained, never valued his literary criticism except in terms of its immediate impact. 'Much of the *permanence* of Mr Pound's criticism', he argued, 'is due simply to his having seen so clearly what needed to be said at a particular time; his occupation with his own moment and its needs has led him to say many things which are of permanent value.'[4] Pound and Eliot were the pioneers of the twentieth-century revolution in poetry. Like Wordsworth before them, they were bound to attack

some venerated names. Wordsworth attacked Pope; Pound
attacked Milton. But the real point of attack, as Eliot made
clear, was not so much Milton and his work as 'the idolatry
of a great artist by unintelligent critics, and his imitation by
uninspired practitioners'.[5] The situation of English poetry
about the year 1910 seemed urgently to demand the rejection
of Milton's prepotence: Eliot and Pound, through their poetry
as well as their criticism, began to effect his dislodgement.
Largely as a result of Eliot's great and increasing prestige as
a poet and critic, the 'twenties saw a marked decline in Milton's
reputation, and a corresponding upsurge of interest in the
Metaphysical poets. The Metaphysical vogue, like the questioning of Milton's status, had a great deal to do with Eliot's
poetic ambitions in the 'twenties.

Eliot's early Milton criticism, as well as his essays on Marvell,
Massinger and the Metaphysical poets, is essentially propagandist in character. He used his criticism to justify his own
techniques in verse, to canonize his own poetic taste, to condition his future readership. When he praised certain qualities
in Donne, for example, he was inspired less by the actual
Donne than by his conception of the ideal modern poet. And
when he admired passages from Tourneur and Middleton for
exhibiting 'that perpetual slight alteration of language, words
perpetually juxtaposed in new and sudden combinations,
meanings perpetually *eingeschachtelt* into meanings', he might
well have been alluding to one of the most striking features
of his own early poetry. His rejection of Milton was based on
the belief that of all the English poets of the past, Milton was
the one least likely to be of help to the modern poet in dealing
with immediate experience in familiar and colloquial language.
In his famous concept of a seventeenth-century 'dissociation
of sensibility', Eliot provided a theoretical justification for his
exaltation of the Metaphysicals and his denigration of Milton.
He blamed the latter for having helped to destroy the fusion
of thought and feeling which was characteristic of Metaphysical
poetry, for having done damage to English poetry from which
it never wholly recovered. Later, when it seemed to him that
the modern situation in poetry had changed, that restraint
rather than experiment was called for, Eliot expressed some
altered views on Milton and his influence, suggesting that
young poets might approach the study of his work without
danger, and that they might even profit from their study.

Eliot's case against Milton amounted, in the end, to little more than a temporary rejection of his influence.

What F. R. Leavis, in a letter to *The Times Literary Supplement*, described as 'the post-Eliot case against Milton', is a much more serious affair. The criticisms of the Grand Style by Eliot and Pound, which were really what Bergonzi has called 'the working observations' of practising poets, were valid for their place and time. Eliot would never have thought of claiming that his remarks possessed a timeless validity. His 'workshop criticism' had its justification in that it helped to produce great modern poetry. But since the situation in poetry is constantly changing, Eliot's kind of criticism, with its emphasis on the goodness or badness of a poet's influence on other poets, can never remain valid for very long. The post-Eliot attack on Milton is not so modest in its scope. For one thing, not just Milton's influence, but what Leavis calls 'the whole Miltonic habit as given in the Miltonic use of language' is in question.[6] Althought it is almost certainly true that without Eliot there would have been no serious questioning of Milton's major status, his remarks on Milton's style now seem relatively unimportant: they belong to literary history rather than to literary criticism. But for many readers and critics, Leavis's attack on the Grand Style still holds its ground. Donald Davie speaks for them when he claims that Leavis's account of the style of *Paradise Lost* 'seems more clearly just on each new reading'.[7] Apart from Leavis's three essays on Milton's style—one in *Revaluation* and the others in *The Common Pursuit*—the other major element in the Milton Controversy is A. J. A. Waldock's analysis of the structure of the epic in his book *'Paradise Lost' and its Critics*. Here Waldock tries to demonstrate Milton's incompetence in assessing and dealing with narrative problems, and suggests that *Paradise Lost* suffers from serious discords at its very centre, the reader's response often being in conflict with Milton's intention.

There are few really original elements in the modern attack on Milton and his work. Most of the arguments are merely developments of earlier strictures, or inversions of earlier praises. Waldock's attack on the structure of the epic and his diagnosis of a conflict of values in the poem are foreshadowed in Bagehot's review of Masson's *Life* (1859), and in Raleigh's book on Milton (1900). Nor is there anything particularly modern about criticisms of Milton's influence on other poets.

In his *Postscript to the Odyssey* (1723), Pope wrote of the dangers involved in trying to imitate the style of *Paradise Lost:* the imitators, he suggested, were 'a hundred times more obsolete and cramp' than their original. Even the modern complaints about the intrinsic deficiencies of the Grand Style are not really new: modern critics often selected for censure the very qualities which earlier critics had selected for praise, but they did not present anything like a new account of the properties of the epic verse. As James Thorpe points out, 'artificiality, in the language of the earlier critics, was used as a characteristic; now, having become a sin, it was the basis for the condemnation of the style'.[8] And finally, the antipathy towards Milton the man and towards his ideas, so frequently encountered in twentieth-century criticism, can be traced as far back as the seventeenth century. Modern critics who complained about the poverty of Milton's thought were not being very original: the nineteenth century had, on the whole, presented him as singularly lacking in intellectual power, as a sullen Puritan of narrow outlook and bigoted views; critics from Shelley to Sir Walter Raleigh had regarded his greatest poem as a monument to dead or repellent ideas.

But although most of the modern objections can be found in earlier criticism, the twentieth century has seen the first really systematic and sustained questioning of Milton's major status. It has also seen the emergence of what might be called an anti-Milton critical movement, dedicated to undermining Milton's position and commanding a good deal of influence and authority.

The striking contrast between the earlier attitude of approval, and the strong outburst of disapproval which has been the most striking feature of modern Milton criticism, has caused some critics to regard the attack on Milton's traditional reputation as a wanton and foolish assault on an impregnable position. Few of his modern apologists have been wholly free from such a belief. E. M. W. Tillyard, for example, made two suggestions about those who were engaged in attacking Milton's verse. They ought, in the first place, to remember the praise it had received from the nineteenth-century critics, 'a cloud of witnesses not lightly dispersed'; and they had probably not read the poetry closely enough to assimilate the Miltonic decorum.[9] It is not difficult to feel a certain sympathy for critics whose taste had been formed along Miltonic lines and who suddenly found themselves confronted by what seemed a massive assault upon something they held dear. Sir Herbert Grierson admitted his impatience at seeing T. S. Eliot, F. R. Leavis and Herbert Read undertake what he called 'the complete revaluation of our literature', explaining that 'a new phenomenon makes us not only uncomfortable but too often angry'. To critics and scholars like Grierson, Bush and Tillyard, who had devoted much of their lives to the study and exposition of Milton and his work, and who knew that their high estimate of that work had the solid backing of two centuries of critical authority, the adverse comments of modern critics must have seemed little short of impertinent. Douglas Bush, indeed, went so far as to suggest that the modern reaction had made little headway among those who really knew Milton. And Leavis felt compelled, in answer to such suggestions, to point out that his pocket edition of Milton was 'falling to pieces from use', being the only book he carried steadily between 1915 and 1919.[10]

There is no point in trying to dismiss the modern case against Milton as if it amounted merely to a loss of balance and perspective on the part of a few perverse critics who were deficient in real knowledge of his work and who had a vested interest in other poets. For two reasons at least the modern questioning of Milton's traditional position was almost inevitable. His exalted position during the two previous centuries had a good deal to do with the fact that poets found his work a constant source of inspiration. What gave the anti-Milton movement its initial impetus was the fact that for the first time since the beginning of the eighteenth century, poets could no longer look to his work for example and stimulation: after two centuries of predominance he ceased to be a living force in English poetry. The decline of his influence among practising poets was bound to be accompanied by some loss of prestige among literary critics, especially among those who judged the poetry of the past in terms of its relevance to the problems of contemporary poets. The second reason for the modern reaction lay in the character of previous criticism, the ambivalence and lack of conviction that lay at the heart of the work of many eighteenth- and nineteenth-century admirers. Had the traditionally high estimate of Milton been backed by a well-argued and convincing critical case—instead of merely being supported, as it so often was, by vague appreciative comments—

it would have been difficult for modern critics to question it
with any real conviction. That they have been able to establish
what must be regarded as a rather formidable case suggests
weaknesses and deficiencies in the work of Milton's older
admirers. Such weaknesses have made it possible for anti-
Miltonists to imply that Milton's prescriptive title to veneration
was often a matter of routine, inert convention, since it was
not supported by demonstration or cogent argument.

Milton's position in English literature has always depended
primarily on *Paradise Lost*. One of the most influential of all
traditional appraisals of the epic is Johnson's critique in his
Life of Milton. Johnson's verdict was that *Paradise Lost*,
'considered with respect to design, may claim the first place,
and with respect to performance, the second, among the productions of the human mind'. In support of this opinion he
isolated the aspects of the poem which he considered worthy
of praise: 'Before the greatness displayed in Milton's poem all
other greatness shrinks away. . . . It is justly remarked by
Addison, that this poem has, by the nature of its subject, the
advantage above all others, that it is universally and perpetually
interesting. . . . In Milton every line breathes sanctity of thought
and purity of manners. . . . The poet, whatever is done, is always
great.' Johnson's analysis of the merits of Milton's greatest
poem is, as George Watson suggests, 'an act of self-persuasion,
and one unconvincing and unconvinced reason after another
is advanced why the epic has to be praised'.[11]

But whereas Johnson's praises are often vague and general,
his censures are comparatively specific and concrete, and they
carry a conviction that is absent from his analysis of the merits
of *Paradise Lost*. He did not want to be too specific in his
censures; 'for what Englishman', he asked, 'can take delight in
transcribing passages which, if they lessen the reputation of
Milton, diminish in some degree the honour of our country?'
In spite of this sentiment, however, it is difficult not to feel
that Johnson's censures counteract, and possibly outweigh,
his praises: 'The reader finds no transaction in which he can by
any effort of imagination place himself; he has therefore little
natural curiosity or sympathy. . . . The good and evil of Eter-
nity are too ponderous for the wings of wit; the mind sinks
under them in passive helplessness. . . . The want of human
interest is always felt. *Paradise Lost* is one of the books which
the reader admires and lays down, and forgets to take up

again. . . . The confusion of spirit and matter which pervades the whole narration of the war in heaven fills it with incongruity.' Johnson concludes his critique of the epic with the suggestion that, although it has its faults, anyone who can put these 'in balance with its beauties' must be 'pitied for want of sensibility'.

It may indeed be true that the faults of *Paradise Lost* are insignificant when put in balance with its beauties, but this is not apparent from Johnson's presentation of the case. This was clear to many of his contemporaries; his *Life of Milton* provoked angry reactions from Milton's admirers, among them Cowper: 'Oh that Johnson! how does every page of his on the subject, ay, almost every paragraph, kindle my indignation!'[12]

George Watson suggests that the Victorian attitude to Milton, 'one of bored and disingenuous reverence',[13] is clearly foreshadowed in Johnson's treatment of the epic. In general, the same lack of reasoned conviction that we find in Johnson is also to be found in nineteenth-century criticism of *Paradise Lost*. 'What book is really greater?', asked Walter Bagehot, admitting at the same time that scarcely any book in the world was open to a greater number of criticisms. Like Johnson's, Bagehot's censures are detailed, forcefully expressed and damaging; his praises, on the other hand, are too often vague and unconvincing. He writes about 'a solemn and firm music in the lines', about 'brooding sublimity', 'a manly strength, a haunting atmosphere of enhancing suggestions'.[14] Sir Walter Raleigh drew attention to Milton's lack of humour, to the absence of subtlety in his work, to the lack of appeal in the matter and sentiments of the epic. In spite of such defects, and of many others to which he drew attention, Raleigh could write: 'But enough of this vein of criticism. . . . To find him at his best we must look at those passages of unsurpassed magnificence wherein he describes some noble or striking attitude, some strong or majestic action. . . . In this, the loftiest part of his task, his other defects, as if by some hidden law of compensation, are splendidly redeemed.'[15] For Raleigh, the redeeming feature of *Paradise Lost* was its style: he could find little else in the poem of which he could write with the same degree of approval. A critic who believed that a great epic poem ought to have more to recommend it than a great style would scarcely find Raleigh's high estimate of *Paradise Lost* very convincing.

Modern apologists for Milton have been faced with two major tasks. They have had to answer modern objections and at the same time to supply the deficiencies of nineteenth-century 'appreciative' criticism. Most of them have recognized the limitations of the nineteenth-century approach, and have realized that they must open up new grounds of aesthetic and intellectual sympathy if they are to vindicate Milton's claim to eminence. Dissatisfaction with almost every aspect of the nineteenth-century approach has been widely expressed. J. H. Hanford, for example, believed that Milton had fared ill even at the hands of his most devoted defenders in the past, that in previous centuries, 'the mass of critical appreciation seems in a large measure to have missed its mark, to have been, on the whole, perversely directed to aspects of his work which he himself would have deemed of secondary importance'. Charles Williams rightly deplored the traditional view of 'an august, solemn, proud and (on the whole) unintelligent and uninteresting Milton'. C. S. Lewis claimed that after Blake, 'Milton criticism is lost in misunderstanding ... the critics and the poet were at cross purposes. They did not see what the poem was about'. T. S. Eliot thought that Milton's greatness had been 'sufficiently celebrated', though, he added, 'largely for the wrong reasons'. And Professor Wright argued that 'the revulsion from *Paradise Lost* could not have happened without certain weaknesses and false trends in the previous, traditional appraisals of the poem'.[16]

The strong reaction against the nineteenth-century evaluation of Milton and his poetry had one significant result. A large number of scholars and critics, weary of what C. S. Lewis called 'the babble about the majestic rolls of proper names', were determined to free Milton criticism from its obsession with art and music. The artist was not forgotten, but there was a new and growing emphasis on the value of his ideas and beliefs, a new conviction that there was no need to limit his achievement in *Paradise Lost* to the Grand Style and the characterization of Satan. This rehabilitation of Milton's thought must be regarded as the outstanding modern contribution to the study of his work. Another significant modern development has been the discovery that in some important respects there is a great deal to be learned from Milton's early biographers and editors. The work of the early biographers— Edward Phillips, John Aubrey, Jonathan Richardson and the 'anonymous biographer'—has been used most effectively by Helen Darbishire and others to clear away misconceptions about Milton's character, most of which had their origin in political prejudice, and to provide us with a portrait which is at once more convincing and more consonant with the facts than the one drawn by Johnson. And the work of the early editors—Bentley, Hume, the Richardsons and Newton—has provided 'verbal critics' with a great store of subtle and interesting readings, readings which help to dispose of the Leavisite argument that in *Paradise Lost* verbal music thrives at the expense of subtlety and sensitivity.

The Milton Controversy has often been less concerned with the merits and defects of *Paradise Lost* than with the claims of rival critical theories. The epic has been used by critics and scholars of every school to illustrate their own particular critical approaches and evaluative techniques. It has also been a major battlefield in the war between scholarship and literary criticism: Milton's most notable champions, as T. S. Eliot pointed out, have almost all been scholars and teachers; his detractors, on the other hand, have generally been literary critics—most of whom have had little respect for the critical abilities and literary judgments of his academic defenders. Milton and his work have been drawn into literary politics, into arguments about the merits of Christianity. *Paradise Lost* has frequently been invoked in the controversy between 'Historical' critics and 'New' critics. It has been used by Professor Empson to illustrate his concept of 'ambiguity', by Cleanth Brooks and Christopher Ricks to show the merits of 'verbal criticism', by Professor Waldock to elaborate a monistic theory of narrative. For literary critics of every kind, Milton's work is still relevant, still very much a live issue.

In some important respects, the modern controversy has had results favourable to Milton. The adverse criticism directed against his work since 1900 has stimulated some extremely effective defensive criticism, and has also contributed to the extinction of the disingenuous and uncritical approach common in Milton criticism before the present century. Such an approach would, in any event, have little chance of a hearing in the modern climate of criticism, in which no reputations are taken for granted. The fact that Milton has triumphantly withstood the modern onslaught on almost every aspect of his work is a more convincing guarantee of his greatness than the formal reverence accorded to his work by the Victorian critics. Those who desire to see Milton established as 'Shakespeare's compeer, not rival' must be grateful to the critics who have questioned his major status; these critics have forced Miltonists to provide a broad and rational basis for his claim to eminence. An old orthodoxy has been overthrown, an orthodoxy which made it almost impossible, as Johnson discovered, to censure Milton's work without the risk of abuse. He is no longer, in spite of the fears of Dr Leavis, 'the keep of an anti-critical defensive system', or even a 'massive central part of the establishment'.[17] Critics can now record their dislike for Milton and his work without fear of universal ridicule; in some quarters, in fact, it has become distinctly unfashionable to express any marked enthusiasm for *Paradise Lost*.

Later generations of critics and historians may wonder at the fact that the Milton criticism of the present century has been so markedly controversial in character; they may also wonder at the amount of time and energy devoted by Miltonists to answering in detail almost every criticism made by Eliot, Pound, Read, Leavis and Waldock. By taking the remarks of these critics with such seriousness, it may well be felt, we are giving them an undue eminence. The fact is, however, that hardly anybody has been able to write about Milton's poetry since the early 'thirties without in some way becoming involved in the modern controversy. Even if it only marks a passing phase in the history of Milton's reputation, for modern readers of his poetry it is an extremely important one. The best work of critics like Eliot, Leavis and Waldock is a record of what, in the light of the contemporary situation in literature, seems to be wrong with Milton's poetry. And for twentieth-century readers of *Paradise Lost*, twentieth-century criticisms are, after all, the really interesting and important ones.

In one important respect, Milton is in a more fortunate position than Shakespeare. T. S. Eliot issued his famous challenge to Miltonists in his 1935 English Association lecture. The challenge was accepted, the expected controversy followed, and Milton criticism received a fresh and much-needed stimulus. In 1919 Eliot issued what may well have been intended as a similar kind of challenge to Shakespeareans when in an essay on *Hamlet* he described that play as 'most certainly an artistic failure'. The response was disappointing: no great modern controversy ensued. Modern Shakespeare criticism is lacking in vigour and excitement; it has degenerated into what T. J. B. Spencer calls 'the shadow-boxing of rival bardolaters'. Shakespeare has become a dead issue. Milton, thanks largely to his modern 'detractors', is still very much alive.

CHAPTER TWO

The Grand Style

Hail native Language, that by sinews weak
Didst move my first endeavouring tongue to speak.

MILTON

But then, the mind that invented Milton's Grand
Style had renounced the English language, and with
that, inevitably, Milton being an Englishman, a
great deal else.

F. R. LEAVIS[1]

By far the greater part of the adverse criticism of Milton in the
twentieth century has been directed against his style and versification, especially against the style of *Paradise Lost*. Eliot's two
essays on Milton deal almost entirely with the Grand Style and
its influence; Leavis devoted his Milton criticism almost exclusively to the same topic. Other adverse critics have concentrated
most of their attention on the style, versification and diction of
the epic, and much of the work of Bush, Grierson, Tillyard,
Lewis and other apologists for Milton has been aimed at
answering charges against Milton's handling of the English
language in *Paradise Lost*. Commentators on the Milton Controversy are generally agreed that the most important aspect of
the modern case against the poet is the attack on the Grand
Style. Pearsall Smith discussed the twentieth-century reaction
against Milton solely in terms of the adverse remarks on the epic
style made by such critics as Pound, Eliot, Middleton Murry,
Leavis and Read. Cleanth Brooks, in his survey of the controversy, claimed that 'the pressing issues have to do with Milton
as an artist, and the attack essentially has to do with the nature of
his art'. And James Thorpe described the two kinds of dissatisfaction expressed by the critics referred to by Pearsall
Smith: 'The first was a complaint against the intrinsic deficiencies
of Milton's style and the second against the extrinsic influence
of Milton's verse.'[2]

This adverse criticism of the Grand Style is important because
the majority of nineteenth-century critics who gave Milton a

high place among the English poets did so primarily because of their immense admiration for the style of *Paradise Lost*. Indeed, for the critics of the period from 1860 to 1915, Milton's position in English poetry depended on the Grand Style and on little else. Art was practically the only thing that Masson, Pattison, Bagehot, Saintsbury and Raleigh could see in Milton. For such critics, as Thorpe points out, he was 'the master stylist and the great, conscious, technical artist'. This kind of evaluation placed him in a high but rather precarious position: the precariousness of the position in which he had been placed by critics who limited the significance of his work almost entirely to its style became apparent when twentieth-century critics launched a concerted attack on this very feature of his work, and thus threatened to remove the great traditional support on which Milton's reputation was based.

At an early stage in the Milton Controversy, Eliot's attack on the Miltonic style seemed far more important than that of any other critic. This is clear from the work of Milton's apologists. Tillyard, Grierson and Bush, for example, all regarded Eliot as much the most important of Milton's critics, 'both in priority and authority', as Bush expressed it. But at this stage, what Leavis has called 'the post-Eliot case against Milton' seems much more significant and deserving of serious attention. John Peter, a champion of the Leavisite approach to Milton's style, claimed in 1952 that Leavis was Milton's most effective critic. Other writers, he suggested, who 'came out' against Milton during the 'thirties have come to seem much less persuasive than they may then have seemed:

'Ezra Pound's vigorous attack . . . now appears not merely cantankerous but vague: Professor Dobrée's praise of Dryden at Milton's expense has been persuasively countered by Sir Herbert Grierson . . . and T. S. Eliot, referring to his own earlier deprecations, has lately been at some pains to point out, in the words of *Prufrock*, "That is not what I meant at all; That is not it, at all". But the chapter in *Revaluation* still holds its ground . . . a reasoned and, in the absence of confutation, compelling analysis of deficiency.'[3] Whatever we may feel about Leavis's essay as a 'compelling analysis of deficiency', it must be admitted that he is the most forceful, consistent and persuasive critic of Milton's verse that the twentieth century has produced. In any modern discussion of Milton's epic style, his views merit serious consideration.

In his brief treatment of the style of *Paradise Lost*, A. J. A. Waldock suggested that 'the facts of the poetry—or at least of the verse' were much less seriously in question than the structure of the epic. 'Critics', he added, 'use different names for what they find; they like it, or they dislike it; they regard it as a calamity, or they regard it as a triumph; but what they find is about the same.'[4] To suggest that what modern critics find when they examine the poem with a view to describing its style 'is about the same' is, however, to ignore the wide differences between the accounts of the properties of Milton's epic verse offered by critics like Eliot, Leavis and Middleton Murry on the one hand, and those offered by defenders of the poem on the other. The modern controversy about Milton's Grand Style cannot be reduced simply to a matter of critics finding substantially the same qualities present in the verse of *Paradise Lost* and then disagreeing with one another as to whether these qualities are good or bad. True enough, some of Milton's admirers do find the same properties in the epic verse as do his adverse critics, and then the controversy becomes primarily a matter of interpretation. A very good example of this is pointed out by C. S. Lewis: 'Dr Leavis does not differ from me about the properties of Milton's epic verse. He describes them very accurately. . . . It is not that he and I see different things when we look at *Paradise Lost*. He sees and hates the same things that I see and love.'[5]

Lewis, however, is an exception among critics who have defended Milton's style in the controversy. Few other apologists for his style see the properties of Milton's epic verse as Leavis described them. The reason for this is that Leavis, Eliot, Pound, Middleton Murry and many of the other adverse critics have in common a tendency, often quite pronounced, to treat the verse of the epic as homogeneous and unvaried throughout, a tendency strongly opposed by admirers of the poem. A characteristic of Leavis's approach to the style of *Paradise Lost* is that he appears to assume that a few selected passages from the epic can be considered typical of the whole, that the Grand Style can be condemned on the basis of two or three passages which he finds lacking in qualities exemplified in Donne, Shakespeare and *Comus*. That he did consider it valid to generalize about the style of *Paradise Lost* on the basis of a few passages is clear from his comments in the *Revaluation* essay. Here he quoted the passage from Book IV beginning:

> And now divided into four main Streams,
> Runs divers, wandring many a famous Realme.

His comment on the passage contains the following: 'But Milton's transfusing is regular and unremitting, and involves, not pleasant occasional surprises, but a consistent rejection of English idiom, as the passage quoted from Book IV sufficiently shows' (p. 53). Leavis further emphasized his view that the passages he selected for condemnation represented a kind of 'Miltonic average'. Having claimed that the passage in Book I describing the fall of Mulciber was unusual, he suggested that 'if any one should question the unusualness, the doubt would soon be settled by a little exploration' (p. 46). Eliot expressed a somewhat similar view of the Grand Style in his second essay on Milton. 'It is', he claimed, 'from the foundation, and in every particular, a personal style. . . . In Milton there is always the maximal, never the minimal, alteration of ordinary language.' The phrases employed by Eliot and Leavis, 'regular and unremitting', 'from the foundation and in every particular', 'consistent rejection of English idiom', suggest what Tillyard, in a reference to Arnold's account of Milton's style, described as 'a style of sustained grandeur and unremitting reverberation'. Such a view of the style of *Paradise Lost* is not confined to critics who dislike Milton's poetry. C. S. Lewis's assent to Leavis's account implies his acquiescence in the suggestion that the Grand Style is uniform throughout. Rajan, defending Milton's style, has a passage which suggests a similar view. 'And since in poetry as homogeneous as Milton's', Rajan argues, 'an analysis of any representative passage is more than usually typical of the whole, I propose to consider such a passage in detail.'[6] The passage selected by Rajan as more than usually typical of the style of the epic is the one beginning:

> Him the Almighty Power
> Hurld headlong flaming from th'Ethereal Skie.

The kind of adverse criticism which took for granted a 'Miltonic average' in *Paradise Lost* was defended by John Peter, who claimed that 'Dr Leavis's criticisms were not directed against particular passages, but against the general run of the verse, the Miltonic average, so to speak, and since this is so the critic who adduces one or two demonstrably good passages can hardly feel that he has disposed of those criticisms. . . . If Milton's average *is* a rather dull one, if we have to stretch and strain in order to pretend otherwise, would it not be better to admit it and pass on?'[7] Here Peter is referring to Tillyard, who, in answer to Leavis, quoted from *Paradise Lost* what he described as a passage of 'perfectly modulated blank verse'. The account of Leavis's Milton criticism given here by Peter is one which it is difficult to accept, because Leavis's criticisms were in fact, in spite of what Peter says to the contrary, directed against particular passages. That Leavis considered these passages thoroughly representative is another matter. He did nothing to show that they were. And a critic like Tillyard, who adduced a few demonstrably 'good' passages, would have offset, if not disposed of, Leavis's criticisms. It is no exaggeration to say that Leavis's whole case against the Grand Style rests on the assumption that there is in *Paradise Lost* a 'Miltonic average'. But a good many critics have been at pains to show that there is really no average style in the epic, and that it is idle to discuss 'representative passages'. This disagreement about the very properties of the verse of the poem is fundamental. If there is really no determinable norm of style, a few selected passages, no matter how carefully they are ana-lysed, can tell us nothing about what Peter calls 'the general run of the verse'. It does seem rather risky anyway to generalize about a poem of over ten thousand lines on the basis of three or four short extracts: to do so is to present a necessarily distorted picture of its style.

Earlier critics of Milton were well aware of this. Pope's remarks suggest that modern critics who fancy that they are attacking the Grand Style of *Paradise Lost* are really only attack-ing the decadent Miltonism of its imitators. Pope, who discussed these imitators in his *Postscript to the Odyssey*, found them 'a hundred times more obsolete and cramp' than Milton, 'and equally so in all places: whereas it should have been observed of Milton, that he is not lavish of his exotic words and phrases everywhere alike, but employs them much more where the subject is marvellous, vast and strange . . . than where it is turned to the natural or agreeable'. Pope censured Milton's imi-tators for their homogeneous style, the kind of style which many of the modern critics attribute to *Paradise Lost*; his praise for Milton was based on the belief that he, unlike his imitators, had made use of more than one kind of style in *Paradise Lost*. And Pope supported his belief by reference. He distinguished be-tween two main styles to be found throughout the poem: the 'unusual style', marked by 'exotic words and phrases', generally employed in 'the descriptions and in the imaging and picturesque parts'; and a totally different kind of style, 'the character of which is simplicity and purity', and in which 'we find not an antiquated, affected, or uncouth word, for some hundred lines together'. This latter style, according to Pope, is exemplified 'in his fifth book, the latter part of the eighth, the former of the tenth and eleventh books, and in the narration of Michael in the twelfth'.

Pope's distinction, which makes nonsense of talk about homogeneity and the 'Miltonic average', has been echoed by other critics. Hanford, for example, who pointed out that after Book Three the similes begin to fall off in number, suggested that this ought to direct our attention to the fact that in *Paradise Lost* there are really two main styles. 'The one', he claimed, 'is abundant, highly coloured, pictorial, figurative; the other direct, closely woven and relatively plain.' After the manner of Pope, Hanford contrasted the two styles which 'are balanced fairly evenly' in the poem. Hell, Satan, Chaos, the Garden: these 'are objects of a style brilliant with the wealth of Oromus or of Ind'. On the other hand there are such things as the dialogue in Hell, the Council in Heaven, Satan's or Adam's self-communion, which, as Hanford points out, are couched 'in a language relatively plain, but full of lofty dignity'.[8] Many other Miltonists believed that Eliot and Leavis had not fairly described the facts of the epic style. Professor Wright challenged Eliot's view that 'in Milton there is always the maximal, never the minimal, alteration of ordinary language'. He claimed that Eliot's account of Milton's style 'is what he fancies it ought to be, and what it must be to justify his theme, his *apologia*; there is no attempt to check back, to test his argument against the text.'[9] Like Wright, Professor Summers argued that the adverse critics' description of the epic style had little warrant in the text itself. 'When critics make generalizations', he suggested, 'about the Miltonic style of *Paradise Lost*, they are usually referring to those portions of the poem to which they have responded most intensely, either with love or loathing. Actually there are few generalizations about the style which one can feel as true throughout a considered reading of the poem.' The style, he pointed out, moves and changes as the poem itself does: the descriptions of Eden and of the War in Heaven and of the creation of the world differ from each other in rhythm, syntax, diction, imagery and tone. Generalizations on the basis of a few passages can only lead to a false emphasis on monotony.[10]

These various accounts of the verse of *Paradise Lost*, amply supported as they are by reference and quotation, make it clear that it is not possible to give simplified, generalized descriptions of the style of the poem without leaving out important features. To describe the Grand Style, as Leavis does, in terms of 'the inescapable monotony of the ritual', is, if Bush is correct in his reference to 'perpetual and significant variations, both broad and minute', to develop a wholesale description from single aspects, and to ignore other and possibly equally significant ones. It would be difficult to guess from Leavis's account of the Grand Style that in every Book of *Paradise Lost* we frequently meet passages written in a pure and simple style:

> So cheard he his fair spouse and she was cheard
> But silently a gentle tear let fall
> From either eye, and wip'd them with her haire . . .
>
> V. 129–131

> Such high advantages thir innocence
> Gave them above thir foes, not to have sinnd,
> Not to have disobei'd . . .
>
> VI. 401–403

At moments of crisis or of deep emotion we find this kind of writing:

> So saying, her rash hand in evil hour
> Forth reaching to the fruit, she pluck'd, she eat:
> Earth felt the wound, and Nature from her Seat
> Sighing through all her works gave signs of woe,
> That all was lost . . .
>
> IX. 780–784

To a certain extent Leavis anticipated the reaction of critics to his claim that the Grand Style was monotonous and mechanical. Writers like Bush, Hanford, Summers and Wright stressed the variety of styles present in the epic, and showed that an inclusive and just account of the style of *Paradise Lost* would require a body of criticism far exceeding in range and volume anything that had been offered by Leavis, Eliot, Middleton Murry or Pound. Leavis was conscious that 'the variety attributed to Milton's Grand Style in the orthodox account can be discoursed on and illustrated at great length', but he claimed that 'the stress could be left on variety, after an honest interrogation of experience, only by the classically trained'. Elsewhere, Leavis explained his reference to the classically trained: 'The skill we are told of, the skill with which Milton varies the beat without losing touch with the underlying norm, slides the caesura backwards and forwards and so on, is certainly there. But the kind of appreciation this skill demands is that which one gives—if one is a classic—to a piece of Latin.'[11]

The classically trained critics of the eighteenth century did not consider Milton's style limited in its scope and variety by the devices of Latin versification. Many of them complained, in fact, that Milton had allowed himself far more freedom and variety than could be permitted even by the most flexible interpretation of classical canons. Leavis, in his account of the Grand Style in terms of classical variety, was describing the ideal of many of the eighteenth-century critics, who admired the kind of verse that could be appreciated as if it were Latin. But very few of these critics believed that Milton's epic verse approached this ideal. Instead, they censured him for reasons like that advanced by Isaac Watts who, believing that one line in ten should end in a full pause, found fault with *Paradise Lost* for 'the unreasonable run of the sense out of one line into another', as a result of which 'it becomes hardly possible for the ear to distinguish all the ends and beginnings of his verses'. Thomas Gray wrote of the variety which Milton allowed himself, which transcended the 'classical' variety ascribed to his verse by Leavis, and which, in Gray's opinion, gave 'that enchanting aire of freedom and wildness to his versification'. Johnson and Pemberton, like Watts,[12] criticized Milton's verse for exceeding the liberty and variety allowed by classical rules. Leavis censured the same verse for not exemplifying greater variety than that found by a classic in a piece of Latin.

Most of the modern critics who stressed, and demonstrated by quotation and analysis, the variety present in the style of *Paradise Lost* showed that generalizations about consistent elevation and unremitting magniloquence tended to exaggerate what C. S. Lewis called the 'remote and artificial' qualities of the Grand Style. Nevertheless, none of the critics who defended Milton's verse denied that these remote and artificial qualities were present. Having shown that Milton did not always write the Grand Style grandly, many of them were prepared to defend the presence of remote and artificial qualities in *Paradise Lost*, on the grounds that these qualities were demanded by the epic form, and that their absence would detract from the success of the poem. C. S. Lewis, for example, was fully prepared to defend Milton's epic style even if it corresponded to Leavis's account of it as a style from which the complex and subtle play of speech movement and intonation against the verse was wholly absent, and even if, in Leavis's words, 'no such play is possible in a medium in which the life of idiom, the pressure of speech, is as completely absent as in Milton's Grand Style'.[13] In his *Preface to 'Paradise Lost'*, Lewis, defending Milton's 'ritual style' as the style proper to a Secondary epic, pointed out that no part of his defence depended on questioning the assumption that the style of the poem 'is in fact as remote and artificial as is thought'. The same position was taken up by Rajan, who was 'deeply impressed but also deeply uneasy' at Empson's suggestion that the epic style is not lacking in Elizabethan richness.[14] Rajan, like Lewis, preferred to defend the style of *Paradise Lost* as a predominantly ritual style, and did not consider it necessary or even relevant to a defence of that style to try to show that the epic could compete for flexibility or rhythmic variety with Donne's lyrics or satires or with Shakespeare's dramatic verse.

Critics like Lewis felt very strongly that most of the critics of Milton's Grand Style had chosen to ignore a most important factor: genre. In their comments on the style of *Paradise Lost* many of them paid no attention whatever to the fact that they were dealing with an epic poem, and that genre, subject and intention demanded things from the style of such a poem not demanded by lyrical or dramatic poems. Miltonists like Lewis, Tillyard and Bush felt that one of the first questions a critic must ask before passing judgment on the style of any peom is whether that style conforms to the laws of the relevant poetic genre. On that account, many of them felt, with R. M. Adams, that 'nothing could mean less than a contrast of Milton's epic style with Donne's lyrical conversational one or Shakespeare's dramatic one which did not take into account the different purposes served by the different styles'.[15] All of Eliot's criticisms of particular passages from *Paradise Lost* have been dismissed by Milton's apologists on such grounds: he has ignored the context, and consequently his criticisms are irrelevant.

One of the principal complaints made by Leavis was that the Grand Style did not allow Milton to achieve the subtlety and complexity of Shakespeare. 'Subtlety of movement in English verse', Leavis suggested, 'depends upon the play of the natural sense movement and intonation against the verse structure, and . . . "natural", here, involves a reference, more or less direct, to idiomatic speech. . . . No such play is possible in a medium in which the life of idiom, the pressure of speech, is as completely absent as in Milton's Grand Style.'[16] This kind of approach came in for a good deal of criticism. Again, many writers felt that such comment on Milton's style was irrelevant, that critics like Leavis, in making such comments, were ignoring genre. An epic style, it was pointed out to Leavis, is narrative, rhetorical, consistently elevated; it cannot approximate to the kind of medium praised by him without ceasing to be an epic style. The style chosen by Milton—even if it did fully correspond to Eliot's and Leavis's description of it—was considered most appropriate by its defenders to the subject-matter of *Paradise Lost*. After all, we are often reminded, the story does not deal directly with human beings like ourselves. Readers of the poem, as Summers points out, must not be allowed 'to lose themselves in the sights of familiar scenes or in the sounds of ordinary colloquial voices'. Consistent closeness to idiomatic speech would, in this view, be out of place in *Paradise Lost*. Eliot made a complaint somewhat similar to that of Leavis when, in his first essay on Milton, he deplored the absence of 'particularity' in the descriptions in Milton's poems.

Professor Wrenn questioned the value of such 'particularity' in *Paradise Lost*, especially in trying to describe Adam and Eve in their inhuman state of innocence. 'Only a vague outlined picture', Professor Wrenn suggests, 'could be effective in describing things and states of mind never seen or felt, but only to be imagined. Mr. Eliot admires Dryden for bringing the language of poetry near to that of conversation. But what ordinary conversational language could deal with the Garden of Eden with its purely paradisal phenomena, or the actions and sayings of the divine and supernatural beings of *Paradise Lost*? . . . And given that the fall of Man or his redemption by divine intervention are to be treated at all, I believe that it follows that Milton has found in his slowly and arduously evolved poetic language exactly the right vehicle for what he sought to convey.'[17]

The majority of critics from Addison to Sir Walter Raleigh would have agreed with this verdict. A peculiar feature of the modern attack on Milton's Grand Style is that critics like

Pound, Eliot and Leavis have presented as its chief faults the very features which almost all critics since Addison regarded as its chief virtues. The epic style is faulted now because it lacks 'the life of idiom, the pressure of speech'; because it does not sufficiently attempt 'to follow actual speech or thought'. In contrast to this we have Addison's warning that 'a Poet should take particular Care to guard himself against idiomatick ways of speaking', and his belief that since it is not sufficient that 'the Language of an Epic Poem be perspicious, unless it be also sublime', it ought to 'deviate from the common Forms and ordinary Phrases of Speech.'[18] On the whole, Addison believed, Milton's style fulfilled these conditions admirably.

The attack on the style of *Paradise Lost* because of its remoteness from conversation, its ritual nature, its stylization, was accompanied by the charge that in the epic Milton had practically abandoned the English language and latinized in English instead, and that this abandonment was responsible for serious deficiencies in his poetry. Pound, in his *Notes on Elizabethan Classicists*, formulated what was to become the current orthodoxy among critics of Milton's epic style: that Milton had achieved his triumph in *Paradise Lost* at the expense of the natural genius of English. According to Pound, he tried to turn English into Latin, 'to use an uninflected language as if it were an inflected one', distorting the 'fibrous manner' of English, a language peculiarly unfitted for Milton's kind of latinization. Middleton Murry quoted a passage from *Paradise Lost* which he described as magnificent. 'But is it English?', he asked. Eliot approved of Johnson's charge that Milton 'wrote no language', and claimed that 'every distortion of construction, the foreign idiom, the use of a word in a foreign way ... every idiosyncrasy is a particular act of violence which Milton has been the first to commit'. The most detailed and influential criticism of the language and syntax of *Paradise Lost* was made by Leavis, who stressed Milton's consistent attachment to Latin idiom and syntax, his complete, and 'mechanically habitual' departure from the English 'order, structure and accentuation', his 'callousness to the intrinsic nature of English'.[19] Leavis illustrated his conception of 'the intrinsic nature of English' by reference to Donne, Shakespeare (the Shakespearean use of English he described as the English use), and a 'Shakespearean' passage in *Comus*. Fundamentally, as Leavis later explained in *The Common Pursuit*, the chief difference between Shakespeare (with whom for the purposes of this contrast he associated Donne, Middleton, Tourneur, Ben Jonson, Marvell, the Court Poets) and Milton was that whereas all the former wrote in styles which had 'a vital relation to speech, to the living language of the time', Milton 'invented a medium the distinction of which is to have denied itself the life of the living language'. [20] Two consequences seemed to follow from this: Milton's verse was characterized by sensuous poverty and intolerable monotony.

The charges brought by Eliot, Leavis, Pound, Middleton Murry and other critics against Milton's language and syntax were answered in different ways. Professor Wrenn pointed out that it was not mainly Milton's tendency to use words of Latin origin or in a Latin sense which caused critics to regard his language as artificial: it was rather his tendency to a Latinate syntax, the pattern of which could not easily be understood by those unfamiliar with Latin prose. This is an important point: many of Milton's defenders went to considerable trouble to show the advantages of Milton's latinized diction in its addition of a new dimension to English; frequently, they pointed out, Milton's Latin borrowings are used in his poems with their original, as well as their new meanings, thereby considerably enriching the poetry; critics like C. S. Lewis reminded readers that much of what we regard as typically 'poetic diction' in *Paradise Lost* was part of the common speech in Milton's time. Such remarks, interesting and important as they are, do not meet the case against the Grand Style, which was directed not so much against the Latinate Diction as against the Latinate syntax.

The syntax of *Paradise Lost* has, however, had its defenders, who may be divided into two main classes. One group of critics tended to agree that the syntax of *Paradise Lost* was predominantly Latinate, but they were not prepared to admit that such syntax was necessarily bad, or that it was responsible for serious deficiencies in the verse. Others, however, felt that Milton's departure from English word order was not as extreme or as consistent as critics like Leavis had pretended, and that Milton had not really forgotten the English language when he was writing *Paradise Lost*. Interesting arguments were put forward by the first group of critics in support of the Latinate syntax which they supposed was dominant in *Paradise Lost*. Professor Wright, for example, looked upon Milton's employment of Latin idiom and syntax as 'devices for attaining in English something of the effect of the loaded line in Latin verse, which is a legitimate aim in a poem that deliberately emulates Virgil'. C. S. Lewis expressed another common point of view—already put forward with regard to Milton's syntax by Robert Bridges and Logan Pearsall Smith—when he claimed that 'a fixed order of words is the price—an all but ruinous price—which English pays for being uninflected. The Miltonic constructions enable the poet to depart, in some degree, from this fixed order and thus to drop the ideas into his sentence in any order he chooses.'[21]

There were many indirect answers to the charge that Milton had practically renounced the English language in *Paradise Lost*. Helen Darbishire suggested that Milton's language remains alive, 'is not throttled by learned words', because he is not pedantic in his pursuit of them. He echoes Virgil's phrase about the poet's love of the Muses: *ingenti percussus amore*, but, as Miss Darbishire pointed out, instead of using the word 'percussed' (as Bacon did) 'he chooses a strong, hard monosyllable—English of the English':

> *Smit* with the love of sacred song

She also made the point that Milton constantly mingles his native English and sonorous Latin: an imported Latin word is often 'balanced and retrieved by a native English one'.[22] Milton is extremely sensitive in his handling of the Latin-English vocabulary:

> The Sun, that light imparts to all, receives
> From all his alimental recompense
> In humid exhalations, and at even
> Sups with the ocean.

In contrast to Leavis's views about Milton's 'callousness to the intrinsic nature of English', we have Professor Wrenn's demonstration of his 'astonishing sensitivity' to even the minutest problems of language, 'his exploitation of the infinitely varied resources' of English. His sensitivity is shown particularly in his clear attempts to indicate by spelling choices the way in which he wished his poem to be read aloud. He sought, as Professor Wrenn points out, 'to differentiate stressed from unstressed personal pronouns by such alternations as *hee* and *he*, *their* and *thir*; and he used the apostrophe in various ways to indicate elision, the quantity of a preceding syllable, or the metrical value of a sonant or vocalic *n* in words like *forbidd'n* (corrected from *forbidden* in the second line of *Paradise Lost*) and *heav'n*.'[23] And in contrast to the view, frequently encountered, that

Milton, in order to achieve his triumph in *Paradise Lost*, sacrificed the English language, we have Professor Wright's argument that Milton's language, in spite of the latinate devices, is based 'on common English, on the current educated speech of his time'.

Such work—especially the detailed studies of Milton's language made by Helen Darbishire and Professor Wrenn—would seem to call for some modification of Leavis's strictures. Leavis, however, did not agree that the kind of case made by the critics discussed had overthrown his own claim that Milton's verse was deficient in essential qualities. In *The Common Pursuit* (1952), he was able to show that critics like Tillyard and Grierson had not really answered his case against the Grand Style; in 1958, in a letter to *The Times Literary Supplement*,[24] he still maintained that his arguments remained unanswered; and in 1960, Bernard Bergonzi, writing in defence of Milton, agreed that Leavis's charges had not been refuted, at least directly. 'Leavis . . .', he pointed out, 'might be satisfied by an opponent who tried to show that Milton's Grand Style *did* possess the qualities of sensitivity and subtlety and expressive closeness to the movements of actual sensory experience that Leavis has so convincingly denied to it; but not otherwise.'[25] Bergonzi himself did not believe that anybody could possibly answer Leavis in this way by showing that such qualities as sensitivity, subtlety and closeness to the movements of actual sensory experience are actually present in large measure in *Paradise Lost*: in other words, there was no real possibility of a *direct* and convincing answer to Leavis's condemnation of the Grand Style.

Bergonzi tried to answer Leavis's case, in much the same way as Lewis did, not by questioning the view that the poem lacks the qualities denied to it by Leavis, but by questioning the appropriateness or otherwise of the formulations in which the anti-Milton case is expressed. For both Bergonzi and Lewis the answer lay outside the realm of literary criticism. Bergonzi, after a careful analysis of Leavis's case against Milton, pointed out that his major evaluative terms are 'expressive', 'subtle' or 'subtlety', 'sensitive' or 'sensitiveness'. These, as Bergonzi points out, are the qualities which Leavis values above all in poetic language, and which, he claims, Milton's poetry lacks. But to claim with any justification that Milton's poetry is seriously deficient because it lacks such qualities would involve showing that they are essential to great poetry: a task which has not yet been accomplished. Most of Milton's defenders share the feeling that the Grand Style has been judged and condemned, not by any universally recognized or accepted literary standards, but largely for reasons based on the personal tastes and convictions of individual critics, or on the acceptance as absolutes of qualities associated with successful modern literary productions. In a very real sense, in order to undermine Leavis's case against the Grand Style, it may be necessary first of all to undermine the presuppositions of his criticism. This is what Bergonzi tried to do. He summarized Leavis's theory of poetry:

'For Leavis, the language of poetry should follow, as closely and expressively as possible, the subtle and delicate movements of actual sensory experience. Ideally we should not be aware of words as words at all; rather we should be "directly aware of a tissue of feelings and perceptions". Effective poetic language should be fairly close to speech, "to speech that belongs to the emotional and sensory texture of actual living and is in resonance with the nervous system".' [26]

Hence Leavis's preference for an 'expressive', as against a 'ritualistic' kind of poetic language. By Leavis's standards Milton was judged and condemned, because the application of 'practical criticism' to short passages of *Paradise Lost* seemed to suggest that its rhythms were non-organic and monotonous: Milton exhibited 'a feeling for words rather than a capacity for feeling through words'.

It is possible to feel that the view of poetry held by Leavis is perfectly intelligible, but at the same time to feel that there are other views of poetry, equally intelligible and equally valid. If, like C. S. Lewis, we view the matter in this light, we must accept his conclusion that arguments about the 'goodness' or 'badness' of the Grand Style will not be resolved in terms of literary criticism; the literary critic must make way for the philosopher, because the difference of opinion is not about the nature of Milton's poetry but, as Lewis puts it, 'about the nature of man, or even the nature of joy itself'. Bergonzi set forth a view of poetry which might well be held by those who do not share Leavis's assumptions about poetic value, or who find his view of what poetry should be far too narrow. According to Bergonzi, Leavis's view 'leaves out far too much. It quite fails to account for the perennial human desire for the kind of art that asserts itself as art, as something avowedly other than the elements of normal human experience, and which opposes and limits them. Such art, normally expressed in a hieratic form or as ritual, offers an escape from the prison which the flux of common experience may, at times, be taken as being.'[27]

Critics like Lewis and Bergonzi questioned Leavis's basic assumptions about the nature of poetry. Others were critical of his attempt to impose 'the Shakespearean use of English' as a kind of standard from which poets departed at their peril. In his lecture, *What is a Classic?*, T. S. Eliot suggested that the English language 'offers wide scope for legitimate divergencies of style; it seems to be such that no one age, and certainly no one writer, can establish a norm'. The 'un-English' of *Scrutiny* critics, Christopher Ricks has tellingly remarked, 'is always in danger of turning into the vague and apoplectic splutter which goes with *un British*'.[28] A literature hospitable enough to include James Joyce among its classics can surely find room for *Paradise Lost*—and without taking the good out of it by refusing to think of it as *English* poetry.

For a long time there seemed to be only two points of view open to critics who discussed Milton's Grand Style. Either they concurred in Leavis's preference for a poetic language which was close to the movements of sensory experience, and condemned the Grand Style for lacking this essential quality, or they believed, with C. S. Lewis, that Milton had very properly chosen a ritual style as the one most appropriate to his subject. This whole situation has been altered, however, by the appearance of the extremely important and interesting study of *Milton's Grand Style* by Christopher Ricks. What makes this work so interesting is the fact that its author shares Leavis's views on the nature of poetry and still believes that Milton is a great poet. Previously, the Leavisite critics had firmly rejected the Grand Style; John Peter claimed that 'far from moulding itself to the curves and stresses of its native idiom the style of the epic stiffly preserves a foreign and unnatural cast, and the sacrifice in flexibility and vivacity is inordinate'. And, according to L. C. Knights, 'the inflexible movement, the formal epithets, the often inappropriate imagery betray the lack of that essential quality that Wordsworth called organic sensibility'.[29]

The work of Ricks is not, however, without precedent: as he himself points out, his attitude to *Paradise Lost* is close to that of critics like William Empson, Cleanth Brooks and J. B. Broadbent, who share, to some extent, Leavis's assumptions about poetry, but who, unlike Leavis, believe that Milton's poetry accords with these assumptions. Ricks finds C. S. Lewis's defence of Milton's Grand Style as a style 'which does your thinking and poetizing for you', far too condescending: he prefers to judge Milton—and believes Milton would prefer to be judged—by Leavis's more exacting standards. His verdict is extremely interesting, because he finds that the Grand Style admirably fulfils Leavis's ideal, 'that it *is* sensitive and subtle. That Milton *does* make use of expressive closeness to the senses when the occasion demands. . . . And that our standards of relevance and consistency must be as sharp as usual.'[30]

Ricks's position was already partly documented in Empson's chapter on 'Milton and Bentley' in *Some Versions of Pastoral* (1935). Bentley, one of Milton's early editors, raised some important questions about his use of language—questions which provoked some perceptive suggestions from Empson. We may not agree with all of Empson's readings, but his examination of various passages in the light of comments from the early editors of *Paradise Lost* certainly establishes one fact: that Milton was far more sensitive and subtle in his handling of poetic language than many editors and critics, early or modern, seem to have realized. Some of Empson's readings also make it clear that reading *Paradise Lost* is not, in spite of what Leavis says, a matter of surrendering to the inescapable monotony of the ritual, or suspending our critical awareness. On the contrary, as Empson shows, some of Milton's effects are so subtle that unless we read his poem with sharp awareness we are liable to miss them altogether. Milton, we often discover, had a much finer grasp of language than any of his critics. To illustrate this we may take two examples. Neither Bentley nor Pearce could approve of the following:

> The Birds thir quire apply; aires, vernal aires,
> Breathing the smell of field and grove, attune
> The trembling leaves . . .
> IV. 264–266

'*Air*', Bentley objected, 'when taken for the *Element*, has no Plural Number, in *Greek*, *Latin*, or *English*; where Airs signify *Tunes* . . . Therefore he must give it here; *Air . . . attunes*'. Pearce suggested taking different airs for different breezes. Both of them missed the secret pun which gives richness and beauty to the passage. As Empson points out, 'The airs attune the leaves because the air itself is as enlivening as an air; the trees and wild flowers that are smelt on the air match, as if they caused, as if they were caused by, the birds and leaves that are heard on the air; nature, because of the pun, becomes a single organism.'[31]

The second example is more modern: both Eliot and Leavis thought Milton's use of language in Moloch's speech inconsistent:

> My sentence is for open Warr: Of Wiles,
> More unexpert, I boast not: them let those
> Contrive who need, or when they need, not now.
> For while they sit contriving, shall the rest,
> Millions that stand in Arms, and longing wait
> The Signal to ascend, sit lingring here
> Heav'ns fugitives. . . .
>
> II. 51–57

Here, according to Eliot and Leavis, was rhetoric thriving at the expense of precise meaning. Eliot objected—and Leavis echoed him approvingly—that 'millions that *stand* in arms' could not at the same time '*sit* lingring'. Both of them missed an essential point, however. Milton, as Ricks observes, doesn't say that millions that stand in arms could *at the same time* sit lingring: he has a future and a present tense:[32]

> *shall* the rest
> Millions that stand in Arms, and longing wait
> The Signal to ascend, sit lingring here . . .

Ricks, by quoting freely from Milton's early editors—Bentley, Jonathan Richardson (father and son), Patrick Hume and Thomas Newton—shows that they approved of the style of *Paradise Lost* not because of its grandeur or its elevation, but because they found it full of delicate and subtle life, qualities denied to it by Leavis. C. S. Lewis had allowed the controversy about Milton's style to escape from literary criticism to literary theory. Ricks conducts his argument strictly in terms of literary criticism, and with the help of the early editors—who would probably have agreed with Leavis rather than Lewis as to what a poem should be—he shows that time and time again 'Milton's style *does* command nervous energy, subtle involutions, tentacular imagery, and linguistic daring'.[33] He has provided the first really direct and convincing answer to the Leavisite attack on the Grand Style, and has also vindicated verbal criticism as a useful and rewarding method of approaching *Paradise Lost*. Future apologists for Milton's style will almost certainly follow his lead rather than that of C. S. Lewis.

CHAPTER THREE

Dissociation of Sensibility

Historians of the future, when they come to write about the literary criticism of the early twentieth century, will surely wonder at what T. S. Eliot, in his 1942 lecture, 'The Music of Poetry', described as 'our undue adulation of Donne and depreciation of Milton'. When they try to account for this phenomenon, one phrase in particular will surely have a place in their discussions: 'dissociation of sensibility'. Twentieth-century critics, anxious for various reasons to question Milton's traditional position, felt that the best way to displace the established idol was to set up some new ones of their own: enthusiastic critics began to give Donne the kind of attention hitherto reserved for Milton, who, it was pointed out, was deficient in important qualities possessed by the Metaphysical poets. These Milton–Metaphysical comparisons have enjoyed the support of one of the most influential literary theories of the century, Eliot's theory of a seventeenth-century dissociation of sensibility. Critics anxious to exalt the Metaphysicals at Milton's expense felt that they had in this theory a powerful critical weapon, because the phrase 'dissociation of sensibility', very soon after its appearance, became widely accepted as the statement of some indisputable historical facts, and the theory which it expressed became, as J. B. Leishman put it, 'a firm foundation for further disquisitions and hypotheses'. So great has been the influence of the theory, and so damaging has it been to Milton's position that Frank Kermode, believing it to be quite useless historically, has argued that it must be demolished before Milton and Donne can be restored to their proper relationship. Kermode claimed that the restoration of Milton's longer poems to the centre of critical activity 'alone justifies any attempt to kill the symbolist doctrine of dissociation of sensibility as publicly as possible'.[1]

F. W. Bateson, in his critique of Eliot's theory,[2] has shown that Eliot borrowed the phrase from Remy de Gourmont: most likely from an essay called 'La Sensibilité de Jules Laforgue.' Here Gourmont claimed that Laforgue died before he had acquired the scepticism which would have enabled him to dissociate his intelligence from his sensibility. Eliot proceeded to apply the problems of a single French poet to the whole history of English poetry since 1600. The phrase 'dissociation of sensibility' first became part of English critical terminology in Eliot's 1921 essay on the Metaphysical poets. In an essay on Marvell, also written in 1921, Eliot explained in greater detail the implications of the theory represented by the phrase. In the essay on the Metaphysical poets Eliot mentioned the high degree of 'development of sensibility' in Jacobean poetry, which involved 'a direct sensuous apprehension of thought, or a recreation of thought into feeling'. Eliot then compared a passage from Chapman and one from Lord Herbert of Cherbury with passages from Tennyson and Browning, and suggested that the later poets suffered from a deficiency not present in the work of Chapman and Lord Herbert:

'The difference is not a simple difference of degree between poets. It is something which had happened to the mind of England between the time of Donne or Lord Herbert of Cherbury and the time of Tennyson and Browning; it is the difference between the intellectual poet and the reflective poet'.[3] Eliot then suggested what he considered to be the fundamental characteristics of the Metaphysical poets, in a few sentences which were to have a revolutionary effect on the approach of many critics to the poetry of the seventeenth century:

'A thought to Donne was an experience; it modified his sensibility . . . The poets of the seventeenth century, the successors of the dramatists of the sixteenth, possessed a mechanism of sensibility which could devour any kind of experience.'[4]

Milton entered Eliot's theory as one of the poets who helped to destroy the fusion of thought and feeling, 'the direct sensuous apprehension of thought' which marked Donne and Chapman. In the seventeenth century, Eliot suggested, 'a dissociation of sensibility set in, from which we have never recovered; and this dissociation, as is natural, was aggravated by the two most powerful poets of the century, Milton and Dryden'. Eliot thus blamed Milton for helping to cause the dissociation, and in his first essay on Milton he also claimed that Milton's work was an example of dissociation, that *Paradise Lost* was the great dissociated poem, a poem which lacked the full integration of thought and feeling, sound and meaning, present in the work of the Metaphysicals. He suggested that 'to extract everything possible from *Paradise Lost* it would seem necessary to read it in two different ways, first solely for the sound, and second for the sense. The full beauty of his long periods can hardly be enjoyed while we are wrestling with the meaning as well. . . . Now Shakespeare, or Dante, will bear innumerable readings, but at each reading all the elements of appreciation can be present . . . whereas I cannot feel that my appreciation of Milton leads anywhere outside the mazes of sound.'[5]

While Milton thus dissociated sound and meaning, thought and feeling, Donne's work, according to Eliot, was remarkable for its unity. In an article which appeared in the *Nation and Athenaeum* in 1923 he wrote of Donne that 'The range of his feeling was great, but no more remarkable than its unity. He was altogether present in every thought and every feeling.' In his essay on Marvell he elaborated the contrast between Milton and the Metaphysicals. The seventeenth century, he declared, separated two qualities, wit and magniloquence, out of the 'high style' it inherited from Marlowe through Jonson. Dryden, he believed, isolated the element of wit and exaggerated it into something like fun: Milton, on the other hand, dispensed with wit altogether and was content with magniloquence, 'the deliberate exploitation of the possibilities of magnificence in language'. In Eliot's view, Milton's work suffered from this predominance of magniloquence and the absence of wit. Marvell had errors of taste, but 'they never consisted in taking a subject too seriously or too lightly'. He was saved from this fate, the fate which overtook Milton, by his wit, which Eliot defined as 'a recognition, implicit in the expression of every experience, of other kinds of experience which are possible'.[6] Marvell was perpetually aware of other possible experiences besides the one he was actually expressing; Milton tended to suppress one part of his consciousness while another was momentarily engaging his attention. This at any rate was how these poets came to be seen in the light of the dissociation of sensibility. To the absence of wit in Milton were attributed his simple-minded seriousness, his lack of balance, his lack of comprehensiveness. The 'unified sensibility' of the Metaphysicals made it possible for them to be simultaneously aware of all kinds of feelings and experiences, thoughts and emotions; Milton's dissociated sensibility narrowed his scope to the expression of comparatively simple feelings and thoughts. Herbert Read, elaborating Eliot's theory, believed that 'Milton was conscious all the time of a dualism—on the one side the thought to be expounded, on the other side the poetic mould into which his thought had to be smelted. The true Metaphysical poet is conscious of no such dualism.'[7]

It was, ostensibly at any rate, to account for the absence of integration, of wit in a specialized sense of the term, of a fusion between thoughts and feelings, sound and meaning, which he considered typical of the poetry of Milton and his successors, that Eliot put forward his theory of dissociation. Shelley was commonly used to illustrate the theory. In an article on Crashaw in *The Dial* (March 1928), Eliot suggested that when Shelley 'has some definite statement to make, he simply says it; keeps his images on one side and his meanings on the other'. He could also write about a verse in Shelley's 'Ode to a Skylark' that 'for the first time, perhaps, in verse of such eminence, sound exists without sense'. He applied a somewhat similar censure to the passage in *Paradise Lost* beginning

Thrones, dominations, princedoms, virtues, powers.

The complication present in this passage, he suggested, in his first essay on Milton, 'is dictated by a demand of verbal music, instead of by any demand of sense'.

In 1947, twenty-six years after he had first formulated his theory, Eliot wrote in his second essay on Milton: 'I believe that the general affirmation represented by the phrase "dissociation of sensibility" . . . retains some validity but . . . to lay the burden on the shoulders of Milton and Dryden was a mistake. If such a dissociation did take place, I suspect that the causes are too complex and too profound to justify our accounting for the change in terms of literary criticism.' In his first brief exposition of the theory, Eliot himself described it as 'too brief, perhaps, to carry conviction'. He could remark with justification, twenty-six years later, that it had enjoyed a success in the world astonishing to its author. Not alone did Eliot's few paragraphs carry conviction; his claim that there was a dissociation of sensibility in the seventeenth century was accepted by almost every reputable critic of poetry for over twenty-five years not as a theory but as the statement of an incontrovertible fact. For Milton, the consequences of this were far reaching: in the view of seventeenth-century poetry expressed in the theory, he was the destroyer of almost every desirable quality and the exemplar of what was least desirable. The consequent attitude to his poetry on the part of those who read the poetry of the past in the light of Eliot's theory was, to say the least, not favourable.

It was not long after the emergence of 'dissociation of sensibility' as part of the vocabulary of literary criticism that various critics began to use it to establish the superiority of various Metaphysical poets to Milton. They did so—and this appears rather odd—without raising the smallest question about the validity of the theory. They seem to have taken that for granted. This situation caused Douglas Bush, almost the only critic before 1950 who did not accept Eliot's theory as a working hypothesis, to point out that surely such a doctrine involving not only Milton and the Metaphysicals but the whole range of English poetry since 1600 'would seem to require a considerable analysis of a vast and various body of writing before it could be launched even as a hypothesis. But Mr Eliot covered the ground in a few pages or paragraphs . . .'[8] In contrast to Bush, George Williamson was not quite so cautious in accepting dissociation of sensibility and all that it implied. He seems to have realized, like many other critics that it was the kind of phrase that is a godsend to critics: once you accept it you can elaborate it almost indefinitely. Whole books can be, and have been, written with 'dissociation of sensibility' as their sole basis. Williamson's book, *The Donne Tradition* consists mainly of glosses on Eliot's theory. 'Aside from the differences of individual talent', Williamson wrote, 'what separates Marvell from Milton . . . is nothing less than the Donne tradition, which gave Marvell the means of absorbing all kinds of experience and of fusing the most diverse.'[9] This recalls Eliot's concept of 'a mechanism of sensibility which could devour any experience'.

Other implications of Eliot's theory were worked out in detail by Williamson. Eliot had taught his readers to see wit as the chief means of fusing all kinds of diverse experience, and also as a means of avoiding the 'simple solemnity' to which Milton was prone. Metaphysical wit, according to Williamson, 'paid deference to the notion that one feeling or experience must be able to endure the scrutiny of another . . . that the dogmatism of a single feeling is not urbane'. The last phrase is an oblique reference to Milton. The idea underlying it was further elaborated by Leavis, who fully accepted Eliot's theory. He considered Marvell superior to Milton in much the same way as Williamson did; dealing with *Comus* he suggested that 'Milton's moral theme is held simply and presented with single-minded seriousness; Marvell presents his in relation to a wide range of varied and maturely-valued interests that are present implicitly in the wit'.[10] Behind Williamson's implicit condemnation of Milton's 'dogmatism of a single feeling' and Leavis's explicit denigration of his 'single-minded seriousness' is Eliot's desideratum that no subject ought to be taken too lightly or too seriously. Milton's 'single-minded seriousness' caused him, in the view of those who read his poetry in the light of Eliot's doctrine of a dissociation of sensibility, to exclude many kinds of experience from his work, to concentrate on broad, generalized, simple feelings, to forgo what Williamson saw as the great advantage of the Metaphysical manner, 'an internal equilibrium that could include all sorts of experience and repudiate none'.

Herbert Read accepted Eliot's theory without question. Eliot had complained that Tennyson and Browning, the 'dissociated' poets, 'do not feel their thought as immediately as the odour of a rose'. Read extended this dissociation between thought and feeling to Milton's work: 'His thought was a system apart from his poetic feeling. . . . He did not think poetically, but merely expounded thought in verse.' In contrast to this, Read suggested that the thought of the Metaphysical poet 'is in its very process poetical'. Read assented to Eliot's claim that Milton had contributed to the destruction of the 'undissociated' kind of poetry which was being written before he became a prepotent influence, and he regarded the dissociation postulated in Eliot's theory as a disaster for which Milton was responsible: 'If we turn to a contemporary of Donne's—to George Chapman—we discover an even better augury of what the Metaphysical poets might be. It would, in fact, be difficult to exaggerate the wealth of possibilities that came into existence with Chapman's individual poetry; but after Chapman came Milton, destroying this indigenous growth.'[11]

And so it went on: one after another critics rang the changes on 'dissociation of sensibility'. To Leavis, 'the laboured, pedantic artifice of the diction' of *Paradise Lost* suggested that Milton seemed 'to be focusing rather upon words than upon perceptions, sensations or things'. This distinction between 'words' and 'things' corresponds to Eliot's theory of a dissociation between thought and feeling. Leavis repeated the argument used by all supporters of the theory: that Metaphysical wit saved the Metaphysicals and some other poets from the solemnity which overtook Milton: 'Seriousness for Pope, for the Metaphysicals, for Shakespeare, was not the sustained, simple solemnity it tended to be identified with in the nineteenth century; it might include among its varied and disparate tones the ludicrous . . .'[12] For Leavis, Milton's kind of seriousness was identified with the 'simple solemnity' of the nineteenth century. Apart from the fact that he identified the wit of Pope with that of the Metaphysicals and Eliot did not, the implications of Eliot's theory of a seventeenth-century dissociation of sensibility dictated his views on Milton and the Metaphysicals. The same is true of a critic like R. G. Cox who, in a reference to Milton's poetry after *Comus*, suggested that 'a preoccupation with sonority precludes any subtle suggestion of the speaking voice; the pattern of sound is elaborated in a much broader and less direct relation to the meaning than in Comus's temptation speech'.[13] This comment shows two influences. Eliot's theory is clearly present in the suggested dissociation of sound and meaning in Milton's later poetry. The significance of the reference to *Comus* can be traced to Leavis who argued, in his chapter on Milton in *Revaluation* that *Comus* was the most 'Metaphysical', the least 'dissociated' of Milton's poems.

The critics discussed so far were generally recognized as 'anti-Miltonists' and their use of Eliot's theory as a critical weapon against Milton is not really surprising. What is really surprising, however, is the fact that a great many scholars and critics, some without any interest in the Milton Controversy and others who were identified as ardent Miltonists, accepted Eliot's theory of a seventeenth-century dissociation of sensibility as an established fact: they did not seem to require any evidence in its support beyond the few passages from four poets quoted by Eliot and the Great Man's *ipse dixit*. Even to launch such a theory as a hypothesis would, as Bush pointed out, seem to require detailed analysis of a vast amount of literary work. Many critics were satisfied instead with a few paragraphs from Eliot. Well might Bush quote Johnson's exclamation about Goldsmith's debts: 'Was ever poet so trusted before?'

Our surprise grows as we examine some of the reactions

of critics and scholars to 'dissociation of sensibility'. Tillyard, writing in 1930, would not accept Eliot's contention that Milton had helped to cause the dissociation, but he made it quite clear that he did not question the validity of the theory: 'This theory initiated by Mr T. S. Eliot', Tillyard wrote, 'is perhaps the most suggestive and influential that has been recently propounded in the sphere of English literary criticism. If I attempt partially to dissociate Milton from it, I do not wish to imply that I necessarily question its general validity.'[14] Basil Willey, in what has become one of the standard works on the history of seventeenth-century thought, accepted Eliot's theory as if it were a statement of fact, and helped to consolidate its already considerable prestige by adducing evidence in its support. 'The Cartesian spirit', he suggested, 'made for the sharper separation of the spheres of prose and poetry, and thereby hastened that "dissociation of sensibility" which Mr Eliot has remarked as having set in after the time of the Metaphysical poets. The cleavage then began to appear . . . between "values" and "facts"; between what you *felt* as a human being or as a poet, and what you *thought* as a man of sense . . .'[15] Willey provided a further gloss on Eliot's theory when he wrote of Sir Thomas Browne that he had 'what Mr T. S. Eliot has called the "unified sensibility" of the "metaphysicals". . . . It meant the capacity to live in divided and distinguished worlds, and to pass freely to and fro between one and another, to be capable of many and varied responses to experience, instead of being confined to a few stereotyped ones.'[16]

Willey's whole book is a striking testimony to the success achieved by Eliot's theory in a comparatively short time. But the most striking testimony of all is surely to be found in an essay by L. C. Knights entitled 'Bacon and the Seventeenth-Century Dissociation of Sensibility', which first appeared in 1943. The very title of this essay illustrates, in the most effective way possible, how completely its author had accepted Eliot's phrase as the statement of a fact, and consequently as a safe basis for further disquisitions on seventeenth-century matters. This impression is confirmed by reading the essay. Knights treats the dissociation as if it had been a precise historical event, almost like the English Civil War: 'It is', he tells us, 'as a contribution to our understanding of the seventeenth-century "dissociation of sensibility"—from which, as Mr Eliot remarked in his brilliantly suggestive essay, "we have never recovered"—that I wish to consider some of the work of Francis Bacon.'[17]

How was it that for almost thirty years almost every critic and scholar who dealt with seventeenth-century literature found Eliot's theory of a seventeenth-century dissociation of sensibility so attractive, so irresistible? Frank Kermode offered three main explanations for the widespread and unreserved acceptance of Eliot's reading of literary history. He explained the success of the theory of a *seventeenth*-century dissociation (other writers had similar theories but they did not involve a seventeenth-century catastrophe) first of all in terms of 'Mr Eliot's extraordinary persuasiveness'. He pointed out too that 'the theory was attractive because it gave design and simplicity to history'. Finally he mentioned the fact that 'by 1947 almost every conceivable aspect of seventeenth-century life had been examined by scholars anxious to validate the concept'.[18] The obvious anxiety of critics and historians to 'validate the concept' suggests that they found its chief merit in the almost endless possibilities it seemed to offer them in their treatment of literature and literary history. This aspect of the thing is somewhat reminiscent of the appeal of Empson's analysis of ambiguities.

It is interesting to watch the critics and scholars at work confirming, corroborating, substantiating—but never questioning—Eliot's theory. Leavis's discussion shows that he did not believe that it required proof; the object of the research he suggested was to account for the 'dissociation', not to show that there had been one: 'A serious attempt to account for the "dissociation of sensibility", Leavis suggested, would turn into a discussion of the great change that came over English civilization in the seventeenth century. . . . Social, economic and political history, the Royal Society, Hobbes, intellectual and cultural history in general—a great and complex variety of considerations would be involved.'[19] Leavis himself did not undertake this generously inclusive programme of research; he did, however, like Herbert Read, assent fully to Eliot's early claim that the 'dissociation' was very largely due to Milton and Dryden: 'Dryden is the voice of his age and may be said to have, in that sense, responsibility. And even without reference forward to the eighteenth century the coupling of his name with Milton's can be readily justified.'[20] The programme suggested by Leavis in *Revaluation*, which appeared in 1936, had been partly undertaken before that. Willey's suggestion of Cartesianism as a cause, made in 1934, has already been quoted. Willey's book, *The Seventeenth-Century Background* deals in some detail with many of the considerations put forward by Leavis: the Royal Society, Hobbes, intellectual history. Later contributors to the subject developed the hints thrown out by pioneers like Willey and Leavis. In 1938 Professor de Sola Pinto also discussed Cartesianism as a possible cause and concluded that it was 'one of the forces' that led to the dissociation of sensibility. 'In Shakespeare, Donne and Browne', he claimed, 'thinking and feeling are blended together in a single process. As the seventeenth century went on, and the influence of Descartes began to be felt, this kind of writing became impossible.'[21] The list of possible causes was continually augmented: L. C. Knights considered Bacon's work and found that its whole trend 'is to encourage the relegation of instinctive and emotional life to a sphere separate from and inferior to the sphere of "thought" and practical activity.'[22] He went on to suggest that the history of the dissociation might be studied in the literature of the eighteenth century.

In 1947, in his second lecture on Milton, Eliot suggested that the causes of the dissociation of sensibility were too complex and profound 'to justify our accounting for the change in terms of literary criticism'. Some time before this, however, the theory had acquired a significance outside the realm of literary criticism, until the poets—above all Milton and the Metaphysicals—whose characteristics it was supposed to illustrate, were often obscured. In 1952 there appeared in *Scrutiny* an article by Harold Wendell Smith, apparently inspired by Eliot's hint in the second Milton lecture that to account for the dissociation of sensibility, 'we may dig and dig until we get to a depth at which words and concepts fail us'. Smith suggested that 'the full and effective development' of dissociation must be sought after the Civil War, and he found the economic approach a useful one: Tawney's *Religion and the Rise of Capitalism* provided valuable insights. This is typical of Smith's approach:

'Thus the Puritan merchant's prosperous progress in the world of money and goods was viewed as encouraging evidence of salvation in the world of the spirit to come. . . . There was, then, really a compulsion to succeed, on the purely theological grounds of contentment over the state of one's spirit or soul.

. . . And with this reconciliation of the disparate realms of spirit and matter, the struggle to "unify" them which we have seen in Donne and his associates perforce ceases entirely, since it is quite out of place.'[23]

From 1921 until 1937 no critic thought of questioning in any way the complete validity of Eliot's theory. F. W. Bateson, who wrote one of the first unfavourable critiques of 'dissociation of sensibility'—in *Essays in Criticism*, 1952—pointed out that with the exception of Eliot himself and Professor Dobrée, few English critics had commented adversely on Eliot's theory before 1952. Bateson mentioned a 'faintly hostile comment' on the first page of Grierson's *Milton and Wordsworth*, 1937. Until 1946 no critic examined the basis of the theory in a fundamental way: in that year Professor Dobrée made what Bateson described as 'the first outright attack' upon Eliot's doctrine. That this doctrine was accepted without question for twenty-five years is a fact of major importance in Milton criticism. As long as it enjoyed universal acceptance, Milton was bound to suffer from the kind of criticism it engendered: he automatically appeared in a less favourable light than the 'undissociated' Metaphysicals.

When 'dissociation of sensibility' began to be subjected to serious examination and criticism, it soon became evident that critics who had accepted it without question for so long as a solid basis for their seventeenth-century criticisms would have to revise a great deal of their work and reconsider much of their thinking on seventeenth-century literature. Since 1946 Eliot's doctrine has been undermined in so many different ways that its survival as a major part of English critical terminology seems only a matter of time, although it must be said that some critics are still trying to prolong its life. The process hastening Milton's liberation from the adverse criticism based on the acceptance of 'dissociation of sensibility' as an established fact began with Professor Dobrée's unfavourable review of L. C. Knight's *Explorations*, which appeared in 1946. Here Professor Dobrée put a number of important and relevant questions, some of which Bateson considered unanswerable:

'The theory is that in the good old days before the Great Rebellion, before Bacon . . . man was whole. Everything was thought of together by a process in which thought and emotion danced together, when "imagination" and "reason" were one. . . . Are we quite sure, however, that the old "integration" was not really just being muddle-headed? And is it not possible that this new analysis may be simply part of the Anglo-Catholic movement seeking arguments to justify its attitude, or merely seeing the course of history through its own spectacles? And was not the change in language far more the answer to purely social demands and the growth of a large new reading public than to an incipient schizophrenia? And finally, is it better to write like Sir Thomas Browne than to write like Swift? or to write like Nashe than to write like Defoe?'[24] Some of these arguments were to be developed more fully by later writers on Eliot's doctrine.

A much more fundamental attack on the whole basis of Eliot's theory was made by F. W. Bateson, who approached it from a different point of view. After a detailed examination of the origin, history and modern use of the term, he came to the conclusion that 'however much we dress it up, the Dissociation of Sensibility cannot be made respectable. It's a lovely mouthful, full of sound and fury, but unfortunately it doesn't signify anything.'[25] Bateson analysed Eliot's formulation of the theory with great care, paying particular attention to use by Eliot, and those who accepted his theory, of the concepts 'thinking', 'feeling' and 'sensibility'. Eliot's imprecision in the use of these terms, as Bateson shows, has serious consequences for his theory. By 'feeling', Bateson shows,[26] Eliot means 'sensation'; he also shows that 'sensibility', in Eliot's use of the term, can be equated with 'feeling', being used by Eliot to *define* feeling. In the key passage of his analysis, Bateson continues:

'A paradox, therefore, emerges. Sensibility is feeling, i.e. sensation, but it is also *a synthesis of feeling and thinking* (the two elements that are unified in the undissociated sensibility). This is puzzling. If sensibility is sensation, or the faculty of registering sense-impressions, how can one of the products of its dissociation be "thought"? On the other hand, if the unified sensibility is an intellectual as well as a sensuous faculty, how can it be equated with "feeling"?' He explains the ambiguity by going back to Gourmont, to whose doctrine on the nature of the ratiocinative process Eliot subscribed at the time when he postulated his 'dissociation of sensibility'. In *Le Problème du Style* Gourmont wrote: '*Le raisonnement au moyen d'images sensorielles est beaucoup plus facile et beaucoup plus sûr que le raisonnement par idées. . . .*' What Eliot did, in his theory of dissociation, was, as Bateson pointed out, to apply Gourmont's analysis 'of the mental processes of the individual' to the history of English poetry since 1600. Unfortunately for the coherence and consistency of Eliot's theory; 'Gourmont's psychology is a ramshackle affair, and as a metaphor from it *dissociation of sensibility* suffers from the weakness of its "vehicle".'[27]

A brave attempt to salvage some of the significance of the concept, after Bateson's well-directed and devastating attack, was made by Eric Thompson in a reply to Bateson.[28] Thompson agreed that Eliot had acquired his term from de Gourmont, but did not agree that 'Gourmont provides the perspective for understanding Eliot's term'. Instead, he tried to demonstrate the extent to which Eliot's theory 'rests securely on the foundation of Bradley's metaphysics', his object being to show that it was a more significant phrase than Bateson's examination of it suggested. The kernel of Thompson's argument is his answer to Bateson's charge that Eliot's imprecise use of terminology involves him in a paradox, a paradox, moreover, that seems to make nonsense of the whole concept. 'Mr Bateson', Thompson argued, 'finds this paradox in Eliot only because his implicit assumptions lead him to equate Eliot's "sensation" with Lockean mere or pure sensation. In the frame of reference (Hegel-Bradley) wherein Eliot is known to have worked there is no such thing as mere sensation; every psychic event whether a sensation, a feeling, an emotion, or an idea has two sides: a side that is felt and another that is thought.'[29] But this answer, convincing though it may seem, failed to satisfy Bateson, who rightly insisted that in the actual formulation of the theory by Eliot there is not the slightest hint of Bradley's doctrine: in Eliot's formulation feeling ('sensibility') *precedes* thought; it is separate from thought and prior to it. Only by ignoring Eliot's own words could Thompson inject sense into 'dissociation of sensibility'.

J. B. Leishman's approach to 'dissociation of sensibility' was entirely different from Bateson's, but in the end it proved even more damaging to the prestige of Eliot's theory. Leishman, in his study of Donne, *The Monarch of Wit*, examined some of Donne's poems in the light of Eliot's claim that 'a thought to Donne was an experience; it modified his sensibility'. In order to test the validity of Eliot's claim, Leishman selected *The Autumnall*, a poem about Mrs Herbert. He selected this poem because Walton, in his *Life of Donne*, left an account of Donne's sensibility towards Mrs Herbert, part of which is as follows: 'This amity was not an amity that polluted their souls but an amity made up of a chain of suitable inclinations and virtues . . . or an amity indeed more like that of St Hierom and St Paula.' Leishman's verdict on Eliot's claim that Donne's thoughts modified his sensibility may seem harsh, but as far as *The Autumnall* is concerned there is a good deal of justice in it:

'Well, if Donne's sensibility towards Mrs Herbert was as great as Walton would have us suppose . . . his thoughts, such ingenious thoughts as that her wrinkles are love's graves and that Xerxes loved a plane tree because of its age, seem not so much to have modified that sensibility, as, for the time being, to have suppressed it, or to have escaped from it into a kind of void. Certainly, in this poem at any rate, his sensibility seems only very occasionally to modify his thought, which . . . might as well be directed on a broomstick. . . . To call such thoughts experiences . . . is surely the very opposite of the truth.'[30]

Leishman showed that what was true of the poem on Mrs Herbert was also true of many other Donne poems, and that when he formulated his theory he was probably thinking of certain things in *Songs and Sonnets*, *Anniversaries*, and *Divine Poems*. He made another interesting and important point when he suggested that in 1921 Eliot's knowledge of the Metaphysical poets probably did not extend much farther than Grierson's anthology: if this is true, then it means that in 1921 he knew the Metaphysicals only at their best and in his theory of dissociation he was generalizing about them on the basis of a few anthology pieces. Leishman pointed to the impropriety of basing upon a few such unrepresentative pieces, 'large generalizations about the differences between the poetry of the early seventeenth century and that of later periods'. People who, on the strength of Eliot's theory, still generalize about the 'unified sensibility' of the Metaphysicals and the 'dissociated' work of poets like Milton seem not to realize how much Metaphysical poetry is of the same kind as *The Autumnall*.

Leishman's findings, which were supported by close analysis of many of Donne's poems, show that Milton, as he appeared in the theory formulated by Eliot, was often being contrasted not with the actual Donne but with a Donne existing mainly in the mind of Eliot, an idealized kind of Donne who was supposed to have been 'altogether present in every thought and every feeling'. As Leishman showed, the real Donne was often very different, Eliot's 1921 conception of him probably being inspired by his conception of the ideal modern poet. The relevance of all this to Milton lies in the fact that critics who have been engaged in 'revaluing' him have, on the whole, tended to measure him against Eliot's 1921 version of Donne and the other Metaphysicals. The work of critics like Leishman and Rosemond Tuve[31] suggests the need for a thorough reappraisal of these Milton–Metaphysical comparisons, based not on the representation of Donne, Marvell, Herbert and the others by a few strikingly successful anthology pieces, but on the consideration of the whole body of their work, successful and not so successful, in comparison with Milton's. Far too often, Metaphysical 'successes' have been measured against Milton's 'failures'. And even as far as Metaphysical 'successes' are concerned, Leishman is justified in inquiring about Eliot's high praise of the Metaphysicals: 'Does there not remain some gap between his praises and even their finest achievements?'[32]

Another aspect of 'dissociation of sensibility' is raised by Professor Dobrée's question whether it is better to write like Sir Thomas Browne and Nashe (according to Eliot's theory 'undissociated' writers) than to write like Defoe and Swift (presumably to be regarded as victims of 'dissociation'). Leishman touched on this aspect in a reference to Shelley, who had been regarded by Eliot as a 'dissociated' poet, one who kept his meanings on one side and his images on the other. Comparing some of Shelley's work with that of Donne, the supreme exemplar of 'undissociated' poetry, Leishman remarked: 'After all, admirable as Donne may be at his best, the *Ode to the West Wind* is a much better, a much more poetical, poem, than either *The Autumnall* or *The Epistle to the Countess of Huntingdon*.' This kind of remark is a refreshing challenge to the general conspiracy of critical disapproval of which Shelley has been made the victim mainly as a result of 'dissociation of sensibility'. In another remark Leishman challenged some deeply rooted assumptions about poetry which had their basis in Eliot's theory, and incidentally struck a damaging blow at one of its basic supports. In a reference to the wit of the Metaphysicals which, according to Eliot and his followers, was the real key to their superiority over the 'simple solemnity' of poets like Milton, Leishman wrote: 'I cannot see that mere wit is, in itself, more admirable than mere pathos, mere revolt, mere solemnity, or any of the various excesses Mr Eliot objects to in later poets, and I cannot see why, in themselves, these defects should be regarded as any more evidence of a dissociated sensibility than is mere wit.'[33]

Perhaps the strangest feature of the very strange history of 'dissociation of sensibility' is that among those who did a good deal to discredit it was its author. In the 1921 essay on the Metaphysical poets Eliot had claimed that 'in Chapman especially there is a direct sensuous apprehension of thought, or a recreation of thought into feeling, which is exactly what we find in Donne'. In 1927 he discussed these two writers again, but in a far different spirit. He had been doing some preliminary reading for some lectures he gave on Donne in 1926: 'In making some very commonplace investigations of the "thought" of Donne, I found it quite impossible to come to the conclusion that Donne believed anything. It seemed as if . . . a man like Donne merely picked up, like a magpie, various shining fragments of ideas as they struck his eye, and stuck them about here and there in his verse. . . . I could not find either any "mediaevalism" or any thinking, but only a vast jumble of incoherent erudition on which he drew for purely poetic effects. The recent work of Professor Schoell on the sources of Chapman seems to show Chapman engaged in the same task; and suggests that the "profundity" and "obscurity" of Chapman's dark thinking are largely due to his lifting long passages from the works of writers like Ficino and incorporating them in his poems completely out of their context.'[34] This view of Donne and Chapman is utterly different from Eliot's earlier one—and these were the two poets he selected to illustrate one side of his theory. Further indications that Eliot had ceased to believe in 'dissociation of sensibility' are to be found in an essay which he contributed to *A Garland for John Donne*, 1931. Apart from showing that by 1931 Eliot had lost much of his earlier enthusiasm for Donne, some passages in this essay seem to make nonsense of 'dissociation of sensibility'. We have, for instance, a comparison between the medieval schoolmen and Donne, a comparison designed to show that Donne's mind was essentially unmedieval. 'The encyclopaedic ambitions of the schoolmen', Eliot suggested, 'were directed always towards unification: a *summa* was the end to be attained. . . . In Donne, there is a manifest fissure between thought and sensibility, a chasm which in his poetry he bridged in his own way. . . . His learning is just information suffused with emotion, or combined with emotion not essentially relevant to it.'[35] At this point Eliot's theory of the sensibilities—'unified' and 'dissociated'—forfeits all right to serious consideration: ' 'Tis all in peeces, all cohaerence gone.'

Attempts were made by some critics, however, to preserve the integrity of Eliot's theory, in spite of the fact that its author had gone a long way towards depriving it of any significance.[36] Some supporters of the theory accommodated themselves to the radical change in its meaning involved in the 1931 diagnosis of 'a manifest fissure between thought and sensibility' in Donne. They were able to do so by admitting this 'manifest fissure' but also by claiming that Donne's greatest achievement lay in his attempt to heal the breach in himself between thought and sensibility! Viewed in this light the theory took on a new significance but it ceased to retain even a shred of its original meaning. Wendell Smith's revised version makes this quite clear: 'This yoking together by violence of two disparate realms is supposed to represent a unification of sensibility; it could more accurately be regarded as an artifice . . . which attempts to make some unification between two divided realms, and the very act of which testifies, not to the unified condition but to the lack of it.'[37] Here we see the emergence of 'divided sensibility' as what R. M. Adams calls 'one of the few critical catchwords which have the happy faculty of serving to convey either praise or blame'. It is a bad thing, Adams points out, in Milton, 'when we are told that his thoughts were distinct from his feelings so that instead of really writing poetry he merely versified his ideas, but it is a triumph of literary art when Donne or Eliot anatomizes his own divided sensibility.'[38]

If, as Eliot's theory had suggested, a divorce between thought and feeling set in about 1650 and involved all subsequent poetry, surely the signs of such a divorce must be obvious in post-Restoration and eighteenth-century poetry. But critics who have written about the literature of the Augustan Age have protested emphatically that there is remarkably little evidence in Augustan literature of any such divorce. On the contrary, A. R. Humphreys claimed, 'the best post-Restoration writing does not at all suggest schizophrenia'. To illustrate this he reviewed some of the poetry and prose of the Augustan Age in the light of Eliot's theory: Dryden's satires, 'whose brilliance is that of bold wit working through the concrete vigour of contemporary vernacular'; Pope's *Essay on Man* which 'fuses into a passionately-apprehended whole a tradition-charged philosophy'; Defoe 'writes with all his practical nature, with a speaking voice and the energy of gossip; much the same is true of Smollett, and Sterne's feeling, thought, and style are all one . . .'[39]

Of the attempts to undermine Eliot's theory, perhaps the most successful—certainly the best-documented and most complete—has been that of Frank Kermode. His approach was 'historical' and his account of the purpose, nature and value of 'dissociation of sensibility' is not likely to be superseded.[40] He performed the useful service of removing it from the realm of history (critics like L. C. Knights had regarded it as descriptive of definite historical events) to that of myth. As a result of Kermode's work we are able to see 'dissociation of sensibility' in its true perspective: it is, as he shows beyond much doubt, 'quite useless historically', but it was for a long time an extremely effective propagandist device.

'It seems to me', Kermode wrote, 'much less important that there was not, in the sense in which Mr Eliot's supporters have thought, a particular and far reaching catastrophe in the seventeenth century, than that there was, in the twentieth, an urgent need to establish the historicity of such a disaster. . . . The theory of the dissociation of sensibility is, in fact, the most successful version of a symbolist attempt to explain why the modern world resists works of art that testify to the poet's special, anti-intellectual way of knowing truth. And this attempt obviously involves the hypothesis of an age which was different . . .'[41] The theory which had been accepted by so many critics for almost thirty years as a brilliant diagnosis of an actual historical disaster, and which had dominated their approach to the literature of the seventeenth century, was described by Kermode in 1957 as 'a way of saying which poets one likes and draping history over them'.[42]

Eliot's theory of an historical dissociation of sensibility was only one of many such attempts 'to relate an aetiological myth', in J. B. Broadbent's phrase. As Kermode pointed out, Hulme, Yeats and Pound constructed similar theories, but they all suggested different dates for the occurrence of 'dissociation'. Pound's theory, briefly formulated in an essay on Cavalcanti in *Make it New*, 1934, in language bearing an interesting resemblance to Eliot's, places the dissociation long before 1527. Yeats, in *Four Years*, 1921, suggested a date about 1550. Eliot's version of the myth placed the catastrophe in the seventeenth century because, Kermode suggested, 'his attitude is animated by a rich nostalgia for the great period of Anglican divinity. . . . This period ended with the Civil War.'[43] This recalls Professor Dobrée's view that 'dissociation of sensibility' may simply have been part of the Anglo-Catholic movement 'seeing the course of history through its own spectacles'. It was, of course, more than this, as Kermode's analysis shows: to Eliot, as Bateson pointed out, it had a practical value 'as a critical watchword, a propagandist device to exalt the kind of poetry he and Pound were writing and to depreciate those of Milton and the Romantics'.[44]

The fact that 'dissociation of sensibility' was accepted for so long as a valid diagnosis of the development of English poetry since the middle of the seventeenth century is of great significance in the history of modern Milton criticism. If Eliot's theory was false—and by now it is difficult to escape this conclusion—then for over thirty years Milton was being misrepresented and misread because, as Kermode pointed out, 'the most deplorable consequence of the doctrine is that the periods and poets chosen to illustrate it are bound to receive perverse treatment'.[45] The comparatively recent exposure of 'dissociation of sensibility' as little more than the slogan of a school of modern poets who distorted history to canonize their own poetic taste ought to mark the end of the conspiracy against Milton's poetry which the acceptance of Eliot's doctrine as 'fact' and 'history' helped to foster. Reasonable as it may seem, however, to expect this outcome, there are numerous signs that critics are most reluctant to abandon 'dissociation of sensibility' and all that it implies. For one thing, there are still critics who insist on seeing Donne and Marvell as Eliot saw them in 1921, and on presenting Eliot's 1935 version of Milton. True, they may alter the jargon a little here and there, but, in Kermode's phrase, many of them are merely 'burning the flag without abandoning the position'. The abandonment of 'dissociation of sensibility' and all that it involves is almost the first condition of a return to sanity and a sense of proportion in literary criticism dealing with the seventeenth century. Not until English criticism has been wholly freed from the effects of this doctrine can Milton's work, especially *Paradise Lost*, be fully restored to its rightful place, at the very centre of critical activity.

CHAPTER FOUR

Milton and the English Tradition

Mr Eliot's seventeenth century—the seventeenth century of Jonson, Donne and Marvell.

F. R. LEAVIS[1]

One of the most significant features of English criticism since Eliot and Pound began their revolt against the Victorian poetic tradition has been the exclusion of Milton from what influential critics describe as 'the main tradition in English poetry'. This exclusion has led to a situation quite unique in the history of Milton's reputation. For the first time since the early eighteenth century it is possible to find many influential accounts of English non-dramatic poetry in which he is given a comparatively minor place, or from which he is altogether excluded.

The history of English poetry has been rewritten since 1921, largely under the influence of the poetry and criticism of T. S. Eliot; and the reconstitution of the English poetic tradition by Eliot and Leavis, the two most influential critics of the century, has seriously affected Milton's position in English criticism. His exclusion from what is often described as the mainstream of English poetry is closely connected with the vogue for the Metaphysical poets, which has been a feature of English criticism since Eliot began to write. The Metaphysical tradition, the tradition of wit—with Pope as an eighteenth-century exemplar—has become the centre of many influential accounts of English poetry. This has been accompanied by a loss of interest in the tradition to which Milton belongs, the tradition described in his own words as 'simple, sensuous, passionate'. From this tradition the emphasis has been shifted to what, as George Williamson suggested, 'may be concisely defined as complex, sensuous and intellectual'.[2] The new emphasis on the 'intellectual' tradition represented in the main by Jonson, Donne, Marvell, Pope and Eliot—although Shakespeare and Hopkins are often invoked—has been accompanied by a tendency to write about the age in which Milton wrote almost as though he had never existed. Many critics have become literary stockbrokers, investing in one kind of poetry to the exclusion of all others; the reputations of poets, as Northrop Frye points out, 'boom and crash in an imaginary stock exchange. That wealthy investor, Mr Eliot, after dumping Milton on the market, is now buying him again; Donne has probably reached his peak and will begin to taper off.'[3]

For the majority of critics in the nineteenth century, the period from about 1630 to Milton's death was the Age of Milton. Most nineteenth-century accounts of seventeenth-century non-dramatic poetry were dominated by Milton's work. He was used as a kind of touchstone of poetic merit; his poetry was the standard against which the faults of his contemporaries were judged and condemned. Masterman's *Age of Milton* is a fairly representative book; it deals with the period from 1632 to 1660 and exactly one half of the total space is devoted to Milton's work. When Masterman mentions the Metaphysicals it is clear that he is more conscious of their faults than of their virtues. His few references to Donne are disparaging; any comparisons between the Metaphysicals and Milton are entirely favourable to Milton. Masterman was in no doubt that Milton did well to free himself from his early traces of Metaphysical influence. In a reference to the twenty-sixth stanza of the *Nativity Ode* Masterman wrote: 'The almost grotesque description of the sunrise . . . might have been written by Crashaw or Donne. That Milton should have failed at once to rise superior to these influences which were paramount amongst almost all the poets of his age is not surprising; we are rather surprised to find how completely he emancipated himself from them.'[4] In Masterman's view, the Metaphysicals were to be defined by their faults, 'their etherialized sensuality, strange and overwrought conceits, and careless richness of rhythm'. This was a view which would have commanded the assent of the great majority of critics who wrote between 1700 and 1900. Nineteenth-century anthologies of seventeenth-century poetry were compiled by editors whose tastes were similar to Masterman's. Grierson and Bullough, in their Introduction to *The Oxford Book of Seventeenth Century Verse*, pointed out that:

'In the earliest anthology of English poetry which in the 'eighties of the last century came into the hands of one of the present editors, *Ward's English Poets*, the seventeenth century was represented in the main by Jonson, Milton, Herrick and Dryden, with a few selections from some of the least characteristic poets. . . . The Metaphysicals were hardly represented.

. . . In the *Golden Treasury* it was not very different. Donne appears only as the author of a poem which he did not write. Herbert is represented by a single poem, Vaughan by two and a verse from another; Crashaw by a few lines from one poem.'

It is true that during the nineteenth century some of the major critics wrote in praise of the Metaphysical poets. A revival of interest in Donne can be traced to the second quarter of the nineteenth century. Edmund Gosse traced the modern appreciation of Donne back to Browning, who read Donne's poems as a boy and was greatly influenced by them. Wordsworth's plea on behalf of Donne made in 1833 shows at once his own appreciation of one of Donne's poems and the prevailing dislike of Donne's poetry. Wordsworth is writing to Dyce: 'The tenth sonnet of Donne, *Death be not Proud* is so eminently characteristic of his manner and at the same time so weighty in the thought, and vigorous in the expression, that I would entreat you to insert it, though to modern taste it may be repulsive, quaint and laboured.'[5] In 1889, Swinburne, in his *Study of Ben Jonson*, pointed out that Gray's odes were familiar to thousands who knew nothing of Donne's *Anniversaries*. 'And yet', he added, 'it is certain that in fervour of inspiration, in depth of force and glow of thought and emotion and expression, Donne's verses are . . . far above Gray's.'

The growing appreciation of Donne throughout the nineteenth century had no effect on Milton's reputation, or on his position among the English poets. Praise of his poetry did not involve a corresponding disparagement of Milton's. When Swinburne praised Donne, it was at Gray's expense, not Milton's. Wordsworth and Coleridge praised some of Donne's poems, but neither thought of comparing him with Milton. A contributor to *Chambers' Cyclopaedia* wrote in 1844: 'It seems to be now acknowledged that, amidst much rubbish, there is much real poetry, and that of a high order, in Donne.' The same writer described Milton as being 'above all the poets of this age, and, in the whole range of English poetry, inferior only to Shakespeare'. Serious comparisons between Milton and the Metaphysicals were not a feature of the Donne revival of the nineteenth century.

Sir Walter Raleigh, at the beginning of the twentieth century, instituted such comparisons, and denied to Milton many of the virtues of the Metaphysical poets. 'When Milton does fall into a vein of conceit', Raleigh claimed, 'it is generally both trivial and obvious, with none of the saving quality of Donne's remoter extravagances. In Donne they are hardly extravagances; the vast overhanging canopy of his imagination seems to bring the most widely dissimilar things together with ease. . . . The virtues of the Metaphysical school were impossible virtues for one whose mind had no tincture of the metaphysic.' For Raleigh, Milton was not quite the standard of poetic excellence he had been for Masterman: he found the seventeenth century 'extraordinarily wealthy in poetic kinds quite distinct from Milton and Dryden: in metaphysic, in mysticism; in devotional ecstasy and love lyric and romance'.[6]

Although there was nothing really original or remarkable in Raleigh's enthusiasm for the Metaphysicals, his praise of them at Milton's expense is evidence of a new trend, and a further comment of his embodied a view of English poetry which, in a somewhat modified form, was to achieve widespread influence in the twentieth century. 'The English genius in poetry', Raleigh suggested, 'is essentially metaphysical and romantic. Milton was neither. He could not have excelled in any of these kinds; nor have come near to Suckling, or Crashaw, or Vaughan, or Herrick, or Marvell, in their proper realms'. Raleigh was careful to add, however, that 'our literature is as hospitable as the Hindoo Pantheon; the great revolutionary has won a place in our creed'.[7]

But there were many twentieth-century critics who were not prepared to consider English literature quite as hospitable as Raleigh did, and who placed even stronger emphasis than he did on Milton's deviation from the 'English' genius in poetry. When Tillyard tried, in *The Miltonic Setting*, to show that Milton was aware of the contemporary situation in poetry and did not write in isolation from the English tradition, Leavis reacted sharply. 'In so far as Dr Tillyard is likely to be influential', he wrote, 'I think his aim deplorable. He supposes himself to be defending Milton, but it seems to me an odd defence that offers to rob the English tradition . . . of that unique heroic figure'.[8]

Leavis's view of Milton as the 'unique heroic figure', the poet who was outside the main current of English poetry, was one which dominated many modern accounts of English poetic history. The readiness of so many critics to accept the hitherto occulted Metaphysicals as belonging to the main tradition of English poetry, and to transfer the emphasis from Milton to them when dealing with the seventeenth century, was inspired by Eliot's brilliantly successful essay, 'The Metaphysical Poets', which first appeared in 1921 as a review of Sir Herbert Grierson's anthology. 'May we not conclude', Eliot wrote, 'that Donne, Crashaw, Vaughan, Herbert and Lord Herbert; Marvell, King, Cowley at their best, are in the direct current of English poetry, and that their faults are to be reprimanded by this standard rather than coddled by antiquarian affection?'[9] This placing of the Metaphysicals 'in the direct current' of English poetry was closely connected with Eliot's own poetic ambitions. George Watson pointed out that the phrases Eliot employed in praise of Metaphysical poetry could apply equally well to his own early work, and that the 1921 essays were a justification of his own techniques. For example the phrase 'wit, a tough reasonableness beneath the slight lyric grace', by which Eliot sums up the essence of Marvell's *Horatian Ode*, might, as Watson pointed out, 'be an account of the central style of *The Waste Land*'.[10]

The prevalence of the view that the Metaphysicals were in the main current of English poetry, and that Milton was not, made it no longer inevitable that any general account of seventeenth-century poetry should have Milton at its centre, or that he should receive serious and detailed attention in any account of the history of English poetry. To isolate Milton, to place him outside various 'significant' traditions, to present him as a poet whose work was a kind of aberration from the norm: this was the method employed by several influential writers on poetry. The effect of this treatment was to give him the status of a classic, but to deny him any modern, living significance, and consequently to limit his appeal. In *The Common Pursuit* Leavis put forward his conception of Milton as the isolated, heroic figure. In the same book he very properly deplored the growing tendency to treat the poetry of T. S. Eliot in a way similar to that in which he himself treated Milton's. Reviewing a critical symposium on Eliot's work, he wrote that it seemed to him 'calculated in sum to promote, not the impact of Eliot's genius —a disturbing force and therefore capable of ministering to life—but his establishment as a safe academic classic'.[11] Here it is obvious that Leavis is conscious of the limitations imposed on a poet and his work when he becomes a safe academic classic: above all, he tends to be ignored—or worse still, to be patronized.

Milton has not yet reached this position. The fact that his work and his ideas have been under constant attack since the early twentieth century shows that he has not yet become 'safe' in Leavis's sense. That he is still a controversial figure shows that he is relevant; in the words Leavis applied to Eliot, he is 'a disturbing force and therefore capable of ministering to life'. Milton, as Tillyard pointed out, is not the kind of poet who can easily be ignored: 'He is too extraordinary a person to shut out from our notice. . . . He stands . . . as the perpetual monument of the pioneering spirit in man, a spirit which may have destroyed much as well as created, have caused misery as well as happiness . . . but which we cannot condemn unless we condemn ourselves'.[12]

In spite of this, many twentieth-century critics have either left him out altogether, or given him a comparatively minor place, in their accounts of seventeenth-century poetry. Leavis's main concern was with 'The Line of Wit', a way of looking at seventeenth-century poetry first suggested by Eliot in his essay on Andrew Marvell, which appeared in 1921. Eliot's suggested definition for wit became famous: 'a tough reasonableness beneath the slight lyric grace'. He did not exclude Milton completely from this ideal; he found the quality he described present in *Comus* as well as in Cowley's *Anacreontics* and Marvell's *Horatian Ode*. Leavis presented a reading of seventeenth-century poetry, and some later poetry too, in terms of Eliot's definition. But whereas Eliot was prepared to include Milton's *Comus* in his designation, Leavis was not. For him, Milton was altogether outside the Line which, he suggested, 'runs from Ben Jonson and Donne through Carew and Marvell to Pope. . . . In Pope the line ends'.[13] Leavis would not include Milton because he did not think the songs in *Comus* had, 'in or beneath their simple grace, any such subtle order of implications' as would merit the description 'witty'. Another reason for Milton's exclusion was that 'his moral theme is held simply and presented with single-minded seriousness', whereas Marvell presents his 'in relation to a wide range of varied and maturely-valued interests'. Thus Leavis, described by George Watson as 'the most influential British-born critic of the twentieth century', excluded Milton from what seemed to him the most significant and important tradition in seventeenth-century—and indeed in English—poetry.

George Williamson, who looked at the poetry of the seventeenth century in terms of the poetry of T. S. Eliot, saw the major significance of the period in what he called 'The Donne

Tradition'. The nature of Williamson's approach may be seen in the Introduction to his influential book which, as he points out, began as an essay on 'The Talent of T. S. Eliot'.[14] The Donne Tradition, as Williamson saw it, was the main tradition: 'all in all', he suggested, 'this tradition not only belongs to the main current of poetry, but invites our appreciation to verse as fine as any in our language'. Like Leavis, Williamson excluded Milton from his main tradition because he lacked wit: 'What separates Marvell and Milton, who were so close in politics and religion, is nothing less than the Donne Tradition, which gave Marvell the means of absorbing all kinds of experience, and of fusing the most diverse. And chief of such means was the wit which is so apt at rendering the complicated feelings of civilized society'. Williamson suggested that Milton's work suffered from serious limitations because he did not belong to the Donne Tradition; 'the power of these literary inheritances', he claimed, preserved Marvell's poetry from 'the fate which overtook Milton's when he renounced sensuousness. . . . Compared with a poet like Milton, who created his own literary medium, Marvell is a supreme example of the poet who discovers his talent in the current of a literary tradition'.[15] The claim that Milton 'created his own literary medium' outside 'the current of a literary tradition' is difficult to understand: it would certainly surprise Milton himself, who said that Spenser was his 'original' and who was indebted to many of his contemporaries.

Herbert Read excluded Milton entirely from his own account of significant English poetry. As with most of the critics who helped to revise the traditional approach to the poetry of the past, and to seventeenth-century poetry in particular, Read showed his dependence on T. S. Eliot. Eliot had praised Donne and Chapman and denigrated Milton, Shelley and Browning: Read felt it necessary to point to certain poets 'that one cannot neglect to mention if only to disclaim them—I mean particularly Milton, Shelley and Browning'.[16] He explained his exclusion of Milton in terms of his own theory of poetry. 'Essentially', he suggested, 'poetry depends, not only on the sound of words, but even more on their mental reverberations'. In implying that Milton's poetry fell short of this ideal Read was in agreement with the claim put forward by Eliot in his first essay on Milton, the claim that the complication of Miltonic passages seems to be 'dictated by a demand of verbal music instead of by any demand of sense'. Read's main tradition differed from that stressed by

Leavis because it did not include the Metaphysicals or Pope, but resembled it in excluding Milton. He found his theory illustrated 'by the main tradition of English poetry which begins with Chaucer and reaches its final culmination in Shakespeare. . . . It was re-established in England by Wordsworth and Coleridge, developed in some degree by Browning and Gerard Manley Hopkins and in our own day by poets like Wilfred Owen, Ezra Pound and T. S. Eliot'.[17] This interpretation of the 'main tradition' of English poetry has not enjoyed the same measure of support as that offered by Leavis.

'It is difficult', writes a Leavisite critic of Milton, 'to think of him in terms of the processes shaping English literature, or to associate him with any category other than that which he occupies in magnificent and awe-inspiring isolation'.[18] This sums up much of the criticism which, during the past fifty years, has been directed towards isolating Milton's work from the rest of English poetry. Most of the arguments setting forth various 'main traditions' of English poetry are full of question-begging assumptions. To anybody aware of Milton's great debt to his predecessors and contemporaries—a debt which he acknowledged—and of his influence on almost every major English poet who wrote after him: Pope, Coleridge, Wordsworth, Keats, Shelley, Tennyson, Arnold and even Hopkins, it must surely seem quite impossible to think of the processes shaping English literature without Milton. If we decide that Milton and those who wrote like him are peripheral, then we are confining our notion of English poetry to a pitifully narrow range. Apparently realizing this, some critics endeavoured to make the Metaphysical tradition of wit as generously inclusive as possible. Leavis, for example, extended it to include Pope, and Williamson included Eliot. But the attempt to prove that Pope was a Metaphysical was not very successful: the evidence produced by Leavis in support of the contention consisted of six lines from the *Elegy to the Memory of an Unfortunate Lady*, lines which, as F. W. Bateson pointed out, 'are neither typical of the poem from which they are taken nor particularly Metaphysical'.[19] Against this idiosyncratic placing of Pope in the Metaphysical tradition may be set the factual testimony of R. D. Havens, whose study of *The Influence of Milton on English Poetry* makes us realize the great extent of Pope's debt to Milton. Havens quotes almost two hundred borrowings from Milton found in at least twenty-five of the poems of Pope.

The same critics who stressed Milton's lack of wit pointed to another contrast, even more important, between the tradition represented by Milton and that deriving from Shakespeare and the Metaphysicals, and including Hopkins and Eliot. This contrast is between a use of language which departs significantly and consistently from current idiom, and one which, in essentials, keeps close to current idiom. Leavis has emphasized this contrast forcefully and often: he associates Hopkins with Shakespeare, Donne, Eliot and the later Yeats as opposed to Spenser, Milton and Tennyson. Hopkins and the poets in the tradition to which he belongs often depart from current idiom but, as Leavis explains, current idiom is 'the presiding spirit' in Hopkins's use of language, and he uses his medium 'not as a literary but as a spoken one'. In the Miltonic tradition, on the other hand, the emphasis is on the 'literary' nature of the medium. Leavis and the critics who have followed him have tended to see the force of the contrast between the two traditions referred to in Milton's limitation of the resources of the English language: in their view the poets in the Shakespeare-Metaphysical tradition used language in such a way that 'the whole body of the words seems to be used'. With Milton, it is totally different. 'There is', Leavis suggests, 'no pressure in his verse of any complex and varying current of feeling and sensation; the words have little substance or muscular quality: Milton is using only a small part of the resources of the English language'.[20]

Leavis found those who belonged to the tradition of English poetry which began with Spenser, included Milton and culminated in Tennyson, guilty of narrow and limited views on the nature and scope of poetry. He believed that the nineteenth-century conception of the poetical was substantially the same as that formulated by Joseph Warton in the *Dedication* (dated 1756) of his *Essay* on Pope. Warton found it necessary to distinguish between 'a MAN OF WIT, a MAN OF SENSE, and a TRUE POET'. Donne and Swift, he suggested, were men of wit and men of sense but, he asked, 'what traces have they left of PURE POETRY? Basing his classification of the English poets on his distinction between 'a man of wit' and 'a true poet', Warton placed 'our only three sublime and pathetic poets'—Spenser, Shakespeare and Milton—in the first class. And Matthew Arnold, using the same criteria as Warton—Arnold suggested that 'unpoetical poets like Pope and Dryden composed 'in their wits' whereas 'genuine poetry is conceived and composed in the soul'—considered Shakespeare and Milton as 'our poetical classics'. Leavis attacked the views of critics like Warton and Arnold, and the tradition of English poetry represented by these views. He questioned the assumption that poetry must be 'the direct expression of simple emotions, and these of a limited class: the tender, the exalted, the poignant, and, in general, the sympathetic'.[21] He appealed for a wider view of poetry, for the acceptance of 'wit, play of intellect, cerebral muscle'—an appeal which has its parallel in Eliot's claim that it is not enough merely 'to look into our hearts and write': we must, he suggested, 'look into the cerebral cortex, the nervous system, and the digestive tracts'.[22]

In the twentieth century errors have been rectified, prejudices overcome and the balance redressed in favour of a wider view of poetry than that which prevailed in the nineteenth century. Wit and play of intellect are no longer regarded as being incompatible with 'genuine poetry'. The moving influence behind the rejection of the non-witty, non-ratiocinative tradition of which Milton is regarded as the chief representative has been the work, creative and critical, of T. S. Eliot. Eliot's criticism was always closely related to his creative work: he used his criticism of the poetry of the past to justify his own techniques in verse, to condition his future readership. One of his more remarkable achievements has been his ability to induce many of his readers to judge the poetry of the past by the standards of his own poetry, an achievement which recalls a remark which he quoted approvingly from Remy de Gourmont: *Eriger en lois ses impressions personelles, c'est le grand effort d'un homme s'il est sincère.* Leavis described his own debt to Eliot as a matter of 'having had incisively demonstrated, for pattern and incitement, what the disinterested and effective application of intelligence to literature looks like'.[23] One could hardly think of a less appropriate word than 'disinterested' to describe Eliot's approach to the poetry of the past. He himself has explained that his approach was never disinterested.[24]

The key to the reconstitution of the English tradition in poetry, to the radical shifting of critical emphasis from everything Milton is supposed to represent, is provided by Leavis in the very first couple of sentences of his chapter on Milton in *Revaluation*: 'Milton's dislodgment, in the past decade, after his two centuries of predominance, was effected with remarkably little fuss. The irresistible argument was, of course, Mr Eliot's creative achievement; it gave his few critical asides—potent, it is true, by context—their finality, and made it unnecessary to elaborate a case.' Behind the twentieth-century dislodgment of Milton referred to by Leavis is the fact that, *in his early work*, Eliot could not use Milton; much of the Metaphysical vogue can be explained in terms of the use made by Eliot in his early poetry of techniques characteristic of the seventeenth-century Metaphysical poets. When Eliot's critical disciples—it is not too strong a term—wrote about the poetry of the past they based their approach, as Leavis did in the passage just quoted, on a particularly rigid interpretation of Eliot's Doctrine of Tradition, the doctrine that the arrival of a really new work of art necessarily modifies our approach to the works of the past. Inspired by this doctrine, Eliot's admirers naturally tended to fault or ignore Milton's work, which did not resemble Eliot's for the reason that he could find no use for Milton in his early poetry; as he pointed out, 'the study of Milton could be of no help here: it was only a hindrance'. [25]

In a real sense, the vicissitudes suffered by Milton's reputation during the past forty years can best be explained with reference to Eliot's view of his poetry in or about 1921. Eliot himself has left us a good deal of information on this subject, particularly in his essays on Marvell and the Metaphysical poets and in his second essay on Milton. J. B. Leishman suggested how Milton appeared to Eliot in 1921: 'The example of Milton, Mr Eliot seems to mean, although he never plainly says so, cannot help a modern poet to relate love and typewriting, Sweeney's nightingales and Agamemnon's nightingales, culture and coffee cups, but the example of Donne, Marvell and others may.' [26] Eliot himself pointed out that the study of Milton could not help his fellow-poets in their quest for a new poetic idiom, in the composition of verse that should have the qualities of prose, in the extension of poetry to subjects traditionally considered 'unpoetical'. The successful use by Eliot of Metaphysical techniques in his early poetry, and his simultaneous condemnation of Milton's influence had the effect of making critics who admired Eliot's work examine the 'accepted' tradition, on which Milton was the prepotent influence. Upon the supervention of Eliot's really new and distinctive creative work the time had come, according to the Doctrine of Tradition, to review and reappraise the English poetic heritage in the light of Eliot's contribution, to modify the existing monuments.

The standard used by critics in the Eliot tradition in judging the poetry of the past has, it has been pointed out, been influenced by Eliot's poetry. This approach was defended by Eliot when he suggested, in a reference to contemporary poets, that it was right and inevitable 'that their practice, still more than their critical pronouncements, should attract their own readers to the poets by whose work they have been influenced'.[27] Reasonable as this claim may seem, the kind of critical approach which it encourages has not enjoyed the unanimous approval of modern writers on Milton. His academic defenders, in particular, have failed to respond to the message that lies at the heart of Eliot's Doctrine of Tradition, and have refused to accept the point of view that the arrival of really new works of art must necessarily modify our approach to the poetry of the past. A. S. P. Woodhouse, for example, condemned the abandonment of historical criticism encouraged by Eliot's point of view, and his remarks can fairly be said to typify the attitude of many academic critics. The abandonment of the relativism implicit in a thoroughgoing 'historical' approach, Woodhouse suggested, 'often means no more than the introduction of a new relativism: one reads the poem in relation to one's own age instead of to the poet's. Milton has suffered and Donne has benefited by this new and usually concealed relativism'.[28] Many academic critics, even those hostile to his views, were prepared to defend Eliot's right to exalt the poets of the past who offered him stimulation, and to depreciate those who did not. They found it less easy to accept the tendency of his non-poetical followers to attack the reputations of dead poets on the ground that those poets did not stand for qualities that Eliot was zealous to realize.

But the Doctrine of Tradition was a two-edged weapon, as many of Eliot's followers were to discover: their abandonment of historical criticism involved them in dangers which only became apparent when Eliot changed his mind about both Milton and Donne. His change of mind about the two poets— a change which, it is safe to assume, had a bearing on his own development as a poet—exposed some weaknesses in the kind of criticism he had helped to foster. The main weakness of this criticism lay in too rigid an interpretation by its practitioners of the Doctrine of Tradition, too strong a tendency to assume that the revaluation of the poets of the past undertaken in response to Eliot's early poetry was somehow final and permanent.

Properly interpreted, the Doctrine of Tradition surely implies that no revaluation can ever be final, no dislodgment ever permanent. If the contemporary situation in poetry keeps on changing, as it must, then our view of the poetry of the past must also keep on changing. Poets who a generation ago suffered dislodgment because of changes in the contemporary situation may be rehabilitated today due to the arrival of new work which may modify, in Eliot's words, 'the *whole* existing order'. Where Milton is concerned, the really important question is whether the situation in poetry has changed radically since Eliot's early creative achievement impelled Leavis to pronounce Milton's dislodgment. Do Eliot's later poetry and criticism—considered in the light of his Doctrine of Tradition—provide grounds for a rehabilitation of Milton, for the reinstatement of his work at the very centre of the English poetic tradition, for his liberation from the kind of criticism which continues to regard his work as peripheral and of no importance to young poets of the present? An attempt to answer this question can be made only in terms of a comparison between Eliot's earlier and later attitudes to Milton and Donne—with related differences between, say, *The Waste Land* and *Four Quartets* constantly in mind.

Eliot himself has taught us to see his best literary criticism as 'a prolongation of the thinking that went into the formation of my own verse'. There is an intimate relationship between his poetry and his criticism at any given time. In 1921 he had taught his followers to see in Donne and the other Metaphysicals poets of major importance and significance for the twentieth century, exemplars of the ideal after which he himself then sought in his poetry: Milton was a poet to avoid. Between 1921 and 1931 Eliot changed his mind about Donne. In his 1931 essay, 'Donne in our Time', he suggested that 'Donne's poetry is a concern of the present and the recent past, rather than of the future'. In Eliot's terminology a phrase like this means that he himself no longer found Donne a fruitful source of example and stimulation. In 1921 he had written of the 'direct sensuous apprehension of thought, or recreation of thought into feeling' which he found in Donne; in 1931, on the other hand, he argued that 'in Donne there is a manifest fissure between thought and sensibility'.[29] Eliot's change of attitude to Milton, expressed in the controversial 1947 essay, was much more clearly expressed than his revised view of Donne; since 1935, it seemed, poets had become sufficiently liberated from Milton's influence to approach the study of his work with profit to their poetry. The reaction against the qualities represented by Milton had gone far enough: poets could not live in a perpetual state of revolt, and a study of Milton's poetry might help poets to prevent the language of the time from changing too rapidly.

Is there a significant connection between Eliot's changed attitude to Milton's influence on English poetry and the evolution of his own style culminating in *Four Quartets*? There are reasons for suggesting an affirmative answer: if we look upon the early essays in praise of the Metaphysicals and of dramatists like Middleton as a prolongation of the thinking that went into the writing of the early poetry, is it not natural that we should seek evidence for some similar relationship between Eliot's rehabilitation of Milton and *Four Quartets*? This question did occur to Leavis, but he dismissed it rather abruptly with the suggestion that anybody who could seriously entertain the notion that Eliot's later utterances about Milton had any significant bearing on his poetic development could never really have taken an intelligent interest in Eliot's poetry. Other critics have not, however, been able to share Leavis's certainty on this point. J. B. Broadbent's comments on the *Quartets* in *Some Graver Subject* are brief but illuminating, and may point to an explanation of Eliot's changed attitude to Milton. 'Eliot's later work', Broadbent writes, 'is criticized for the same reasons as Milton's', and he suggests that in the *Quartets* Eliot has written 'Miltonically'. John Holloway has some relevant and interesting remarks on the style and tone of *Four Quartets*; he writes of 'the sombre lucidity of expression going with an elusiveness not of subtle evocation but rather of argument and idea; the acceptance of something like philosophical generalization . . . and the tone, seldom satirical or throw-away, but often quiet, sincere, intimate, unhappy—sometimes reminiscent of the meditative verse of Arnold'.[30] Holloway does not mention Milton, but the implications of his references to 'argument and idea', to 'philosophical generalization' and to the verse of Arnold—verse in which, according to Leavis, we cannot fail to recognize the Miltonic influence—seem clear enough.

By far the best treatment of the Miltonic element in *Four Quartets* is found in Helen Gardner's all too brief discussion of *Little Gidding*.[31] She points out that Milton is very much in mind throughout the poem. In the third movement there is an explicit reference to the manner of his death (III. 179). Miss Gardner points out that the tone of the speech of 'the first-met stranger' (II. 111 ff.), and some of the phrases 'recall strongly one great English poet and that is Milton, the Milton of the close of *Paradise Lost*, or *Paradise Regained* and of *Samson*'. Eliot's lines describing 'the gifts reserved for age' (II. 129 ff.) are strongly reminiscent of Michael's speech to Adam in the eleventh book of *Paradise Lost*:

> This is old age; but then thou must outlive
> Thy youth, thy strength, thy beauty, which will change
> To withered weak and gray; thy sense then
> Obtuse, all taste of pleasure must forgoe. . . .

The close of the speech of 'the first-met stranger' has, in Miss Gardner's words, 'a haunting Miltonic echo. . . . The weight of human suffering in Milton's later poetry . . . and the patience of his spirit seem to be suggested in this conversation in the disfigured streets of London. . . .' Although the full extent of Milton's influence on Eliot's later work merits more detailed study—a comparison between the versification and rhythms of *Four Quartets* and *Samson Agonistes* might yield interesting results—it seems clear that of all the English poets of the past Milton is the one whose influence has the most obvious bearing on Eliot's later poetry. In the light of the Doctrine of Tradition, this ought to have meant a renewed interest in Milton's poetry on the part of Eliot's admirers. Surely Eliot's new creative interest in Milton, accompanied as it was by a loss of interest in those poets who had influenced his early work, ought to have inspired his followers to rehabilitate Milton as a central figure in the English poetic tradition.

Instead, we have the obstinate refusal of critics like Leavis to believe that anything has really changed; the same applies to the Leavisites who have contributed to the various volumes of the Pelican *Guide*. It was natural that the many critics who had treated Eliot's early pronouncements on Milton and the Metaphysicals as if they were possessed of a timeless validity should have felt a sense of betrayal when Eliot claimed that he considered some of them no longer valid—especially since these critics had devoted so much work to producing arguments in support of these early pronouncements. J. B. Leishman pointed out that two phrases, 'dissociation of sensibility', which was coined by Eliot, and 'unified sensibility', coined by one of his followers to suggest the antithesis of Eliot's phrase, 'alone have enabled several later critics to set up in business and to drive quite a prosperous trade as literary and historical critics'.[32] The reluctance of such critics to accept the fact that these phrases, and the literary doctrines they represent, have become somewhat obsolete is understandable.

Over thirty years ago it was suggested that Eliot's creative achievement had provided the irresistible argument for Milton's dislodgment. But even thirty years ago this suggestion was somewhat out of date. By 1930 a great creative period in English poetry had come to an end: Eliot had made his distinctive contribution, and his 'propagandist' criticism had served its purpose by helping to produce great poetry and by preparing readers for its acceptance. For better or worse, English poetry since the 'thirties has taken a new direction; it is becoming increasingly plain that younger poets and critics regard the work of Eliot and Pound as having constituted an important interlude rather than a decisive reorientation. Several contemporary poets are writing as though Eliot and Pound had never existed, and poets of the past occulted or neglected during the Eliot generation are again providing creative stimulus. In the light of such developments there is not much sense in continuing to write of Milton's place in the English tradition from the standpoint of the 'thirties: it is time to draw a new map of the past.

CHAPTER FIVE

Character and Ideas

When we examine what various twentieth-century critics and scholars have had to say about Milton's character and ideas, we gradually become conscious of a rather curious situation. On the one hand, we find Eliot, Pound, Leavis, Middleton Murry and many others voicing old prejudices which had their origin in the political conflicts of the seventeenth century and which hardened into firmly held beliefs in the nineteenth; expressing a strong antipathy towards Milton the man; finding him, on the level of character, inhuman, brutal, hateful and proud, and on the intellectual level generally dismissing him as simple-minded and single-minded, incapable of 'sustained analytic and discursive thinking', lacking any real grasp of ideas, grimly serious but never subtle, ill-equipped intellectually for the poetic tasks he set himself. On the other hand we find a large number of Miltonists, mainly scholars—Helen Darbishire, Saurat, Williams, Wright, Grierson, Bush, Tillyard, Hanford and many others— providing a volume of evidence sufficient to discredit once and for all the picture of Milton's character and ideas inherited from the nineteenth century and still presented with a show of conviction by his adverse critics of the twentieth. The extremely valuable and necessary work of rehabilitation carried out since the second decade of the century has given us a new Milton, altogether different from the unlikeable individual with the narrow uninteresting mind who did duty for so long, and who, if we are prepared to credit evidence rather than hearsay and prejudice, bore only a slight resemblance to the real Milton. But while scholars were rectifying old errors and discrediting old myths some of Milton's critics seemed to be doing their utmost to perpetuate them, often choosing either to ignore or to ridicule what Leavis called 'the ardours and ingenuities' of the scholars. True, Eliot had some approving, if faintly patronizing, words for some of the scholars who had thrown new light on Milton's ideas; he paid high tribute to Charles Williams in particular. But Leavis reprimanded him severely for this exhibition of 'deference' towards the scholars, finding it deplorable that literary students should be required to waste their time on the 'solemn study' of Milton's thought. For Leavis, the question was settled: Milton's intellectual limitations were such that his thought was hardly worth investigating, certainly not worth the kind of attention it has received during the past fifty years.

Leavis made no secret of his contempt for the quality of Milton's thought: he had comparatively little to say about Milton's character. In other critics, however, Milton the man excited a remarkably strong animosity. Pound, in what he called his 'yearlong diatribes', stressed his unpleasantness, 'his asinine bigotry, his beastly hebraism, and the coarseness of his mentality'.[1] Eliot found him unsatisfactory as a man, 'from the moralist's point of view, or from the theologian's point of view, or from the psychologist's point of view, or from that of the political philosopher, or judging by the ordinary standards of likeableness in human beings'. This oracular pronouncement appeared in the first of his essays on Milton, but in spite of its apparently universal application it can mean little more than that Eliot did not like Milton. In his second essay he dealt with the matter in somewhat greater detail. He explained that his own approach to Milton's character resembled that of Dr Johnson: both Johnson and himself, Anglicans and Tories as they were, saw in Milton the great symbol of all they deplored in the seventeenth century. For Eliot, as for Johnson, the Civil War had never really ended. Middleton Murry's judgment was also harsh. 'On the moral and spiritual side', he wrote, 'I find it easy enough to place him: he is, simply, a bad man of a very particular kind, who is a bad man because he is so sublimely certain of being a good one.'[2] Dislike of Milton's character was not confined to those who expressed reservations about his poetry. Lord David Cecil, who admired him for 'mastery of design, for distinction of style, for sustained grandeur of conception', could not admire his character: 'He did not live by faith, scorned hope, and was indisposed to charity; while pride, so far from being the vice which Christianity considers it, was to Milton the mark of a superior nature.'[3] And Logan Pearsall Smith, who rhapsodized about Milton's 'magic evocative verse which brings tears to the eyes', claimed that 'there is little in his character that can make us love him, as we can love almost all the great English poets'.[4]

Even more important than the attack on Milton's personal character by twentieth-century critics was the adverse criticism of his ideas, the suggestion, often repeated in various forms, that his work was marked by a serious poverty of thought, being the product of a simple, if fervent and dedicated, mind lacking subtlety and devoid of intellectual power, deficient in awareness and above all lacking real insight into its own limitations. Again, this kind of belief was not confined to those critics who were dedicated in some way to Milton's 'dislodgment'. Pearsall Smith, in a book ostensibly written in defence of Milton, considered it useless to look in Milton's thought for the immortality of his work. 'For Milton's mind', he wrote, 'was not that of a comprehensive thinker. . . . We read Milton for his literary value, not for his thought.'[5] The last remark poses a problem, and incidentally provides a clue to the motives of those who tried to show the value of Milton's thought. Many Miltonists believed that if the 'thought' was so contemptible as critics like Pearsall Smith and Leavis made it out to be, then there was little point in talking about 'literary value'. Pound could find very little of either in Milton's poetry; he found in it instead evidence of 'gross and utter stupidity and obtuseness' and claimed that Milton was more concerned with decorations and trappings than with expressing ideas. In *Paradise Lost*, as Pound saw it, 'rumble' predominated over 'meaning' and 'content': Eliot suggested that the complication of a Miltonic sentence 'is dictated by a demand of verbal music, instead of by any demand of sense'.[6] Leavis distinguished between 'character' and intelligence in Milton: 'He has character, moral grandeur, moral force; but he is, for the purposes of his undertaking, disastrously single-minded and simple-minded. . . . He has no grasp of ideas, and whatever he may suppose is not interested in precise thought of any kind . . .'[7]

The view that Milton was an unpleasant character and that his poetry provided evidence of serious intellectual limitations was often accompanied by the suggestion that many of the ideas he did express, and many of the beliefs he held were, at their worst, repellent and revolting, and at their best, uninteresting. Eliot expressed his distaste for the theology of *Paradise Lost*, presented, as he saw it, through 'a mythology which would better have been left in the Book of Genesis'; he also described Milton's Heaven and Hell as 'large but insufficiently furnished apartments filled by heavy conversation'.[8] Leavis charged Milton with offering 'for our worship mere brute assertive will'; Middleton Murry found little intimate meaning in his work: 'He does not', he declared, 'either in his great effects or in his little ones, trouble our depths.'[9] Bernard Bergonzi, who defended Milton's epic against modern criticism of its style and structure, wrote that as a Christian he found Milton's ideas and attitudes 'so uncongenial that I have to try to put them out of mind when reading them'.[10] And Professor Empson, writing very frankly and candidly from an anti-Christian point of view, found Eliot's feelings about the theology of *Paradise Lost* 'evidently right'; from his own point of view the poem, 'if read with understanding, must be read with growing horror unless you decide to reject its God'.[11]

The attitudes expressed above were shared by many other critics, some of whom greatly admired other aspects of Milton's work. If the criticism represented by these attitudes is valid, and if the ideas expressed in the poetry, and especially in the epic, are really so uncongenial and repellent, then Milton's significance as a poet must be sought in such aspects of his work as style, language, the portrayal of Satan and Hell, and 'architectonic power'. Those who acquiesced in the censures of Milton's ideas generally adopted this attitude: anxious to defend Milton's traditional reputation as a great poet against his modern critics, and at the same time conceding his poverty of thought, they fell back almost entirely on 'style'. Pearsall Smith's was the most extreme expression of this attitude. 'What the Muses think is of little interest', he suggested, 'what we care for is what they sing. ... Sound, which Pater said was more than half our thought, was to Milton a matter of supreme importance.'[12] Fortunately for Milton's modern reputation, there were many critics who were not prepared to confine their defence of his position within the limits suggested by Pearsall Smith, or to admit that the censures of his personality and ideas by Eliot and the others were entirely justified. The majority of Milton's twentieth-century admirers, belonging to, or sympathizing with, the new school of Milton criticism dedicated to the study of the man and the thinker as well as the poet, see no necessity in trying to save the prestige of the poet by casting the man and his ideas overboard. Douglas Bush reacted strongly from Pearsall Smith's eulogy of Milton's art and music and his contempt for Milton's thought, agreeing that the poet was a great artist, but making the point that he 'did not prayerfully and repeatedly dedicate his life and faculties to the manipulation of vowels and consonants'.[13] Milton would almost certainly agree with Bush, and perhaps apply Bacon's words to those who saw his greatness purely in terms of style: 'Here, therefore, is the first distemper of learning, when men study words and not matter.' Critics who devoted their attention to the sympathetic study of Milton's ideas were justified in doing so. If his only claim to our admiration is his style, then we are surely better off to transfer our attention to poets who also have something interesting and important to say.

It is not difficult to see why those anxious to defend his reputation as a great poet should have thought it necessary to show the value of Milton's ideas. It may be rather more difficult to understand why the same critics should have been so concerned to defend the poet's personal character against modern, and indeed ancient, attacks. Surely, it might be argued, the personal attractiveness or otherwise of a writer can have little to do with the value or standing of his work. But critics on both sides, those who have attacked and those who have defended, have argued that Milton is most exceptional in this respect. 'Of no other poet', Eliot pointed out, 'is it so difficult to consider the poetry simply as poetry, without our theological and political dispositions, conscious and unconscious, inherited or acquired, making an unlawful entry.'[14] A very important factor in Milton criticism is that we know more about Milton than about any previous English poet. It is only natural that bioliterary critics should use whatever information they possess about the poet's life to interpret his poetry. But if the information is not accurate, what of the interpretation? Some of the bioliterary critics even use the poetry to provide biography. Verity, as Professor Wright points out, states that in his last years Milton was lonely and disappointed: his only warrant for this is Milton's description of Samson's lot. With bioliterary criticism always likely to flourish, prejudice against Milton's character can only mean prejudice against his poetry. This consideration alone, apart from any other, justifies the work of those who have helped to distinguish prejudice from fact, and who have provided us with a more reliable account of Milton's character than the traditional one.

The modern attack on Milton's personality and ideas, and the accompanying censures of the subject matter of his poetry are perhaps the least original elements in the modern case against the poet. Charles Williams pointed out that long before any modern critic claimed that Milton was a bad man, that he was proud, or that his subject lacked interest, 'the orthodox chairs of literature . . . had for long professed the traditional view of an august, solemn, proud, and (on the whole) unintelligent and uninteresting Milton'.[15] But while modern critics were repeating such nineteenth-century views, many of Milton's apologists were busily engaged undermining them, and showing that the whole traditional conception of Milton's character and ideas was largely false. Saurat, for example, aimed rather successfully at overthrowing the old view of Milton as 'the stiff Puritan figure', and at establishing that his ideas had 'a permanent interest, outside the religious and political squabbles of his time . . . a philosophical interest susceptible of universal appeal, and fully as important for our time as for Milton's'.[16]

Before the twentieth century two distinct conceptions of Milton the man prevailed. One was the heroic conception, nobly expressed by Coleridge in his *Biographia Literaria* and shared by many of the Romantic poets. 'My mind', Coleridge wrote, 'is not capable of forming a more august conception than arises from the contemplation of this great man in his latter days: poor, sick, blind, slandered, persecuted.' Macaulay's approach is in the same tradition; in his famous review of *De Doctrina* he suggested that in Milton's character, 'the noblest qualities of every party were combined in harmonious union'. The other conception was presented most fully by Johnson in his *Life*, almost every page of which, as Eliot pointed out, reveals Johnson's antipathy towards Milton the man. Johnson availed himself fully of every opportunity for ridicule that offered itself; he sneered at 'the man who hastens home because his countrymen are contending for liberty, and, when he reaches the scene of action, vapours away his patriotism in a private boarding-school'. Johnson, whose whole attitude to his subject is marked by a spirit of intense partisanship, is writing in a tradition which stretches back to Milton's day and forward to our own. 'His fame', the Royalist Winstanley wrote in 1687, 'is gone out like a Candle in a snuff, and his Memory will always Stink, which might have lived in honourable repute, had he not been a notorious Trayter.' Addison wrote in the same spirit, and in our own time Eliot pointed out that he shared Johnson's prejudice. But on the other hand the part Milton played in the seventeenth-century upheaval won him many admirers. In his work on Milton's contemporary reputation, William Riley Parker pointed out that even before Milton's death there was a growing tendency 'to see Milton the Statesman through the misty eyes of political nostalgia. In 1667 Samuel Pepys found it strange that everybody was thinking about Cromwell and singing his praises; but it was not strange, and some of these people, yearning for 'the good old days', seized upon Milton, the most articulate man of his generation, as a symbol of all that England had lost and might have again. Whig interests found him surprisingly topical.'[17] Thus, if Milton's support for the cause in which he believed earned him the abuse and ridicule of good Tories like Johnson, it also earned the intense admiration of Cowper and Wordsworth. As one might expect, Catholics tended to find Milton uncongenial: 'We may feel great repugnance to Milton and Gibbon as men', Newman wrote; Hopkins described him as 'a very bad man'; Belloc outdid Johnson in ridicule, and Chesterton made no secret of his dislike.[18]

Much of this kind of comment, whether favourable or hostile, tells us less about Milton than it does about the religious and political views of admirers and detractors. Unfortunately for Milton's reputation, however, the views of the detractors have tended to prevail, and worse still, almost since his own time, Milton has been the victim of deliberate misrepresentation inspired by political prejudice. 'Nobody', Johnson claimed, 'can write the life of a man but those who have eat and drunk and lived in social intercourse with him.' But when Johnson was writing his own *Life* of Milton, he preferred malicious gossip to fact: his true ancestor is Anthony Wood who wrote the first printed biography of Milton (1691) and who, as Helen Darbishire pointed out, 'began the evil work of twisting facts and misrepresenting motives'. Wood relied on two main sources: the so-called *Anonymous Biography*, which was discovered among his papers in 1889 and published by Parsons in 1902; and John Aubrey's *Life*. But Wood's treatment of his sources, as Helen Darbishire's edition of the early *Lives* makes clear, is perverse. He replaces 'the intimate and pleasing view' of Milton given by his sources with a portrait consonant with Milton's unfavourable 1691 public image. A good example of Wood's technique is his reference to the attack on Milton in *Regii Sanguinis Clamor*, the anonymous answer to Milton's *Defense of the English People*. In the *Anonymous Biography* of Milton, Wood read the following reference to *Regii Sanguinis Clamor*: 'Salmasius was here highly extolled and Mr Milton as falsely defamed.' But he altered this to: 'Salmasius was highly extolled and Milton had his just character given.'[19] Edward Phillips, one of Milton's nephews, described Milton in his *Theatrum Poetarum*, an index of poets of all countries and all ages, as an author 'of most deserv'd Fame late deceas't'. Wood's annotation: 'John Milton a Rogue.'[20]

To arrive at a just estimate of Milton's character, modern scholars have found it necessary to work on the principle suggested in Johnson's remark that the best biographers are those who knew their subject. Hence the modern emphasis on the early *Lives* of the poet as the most reliable sources of information. Three of these early *Lives* are particularly important: that of Edward Phillips, Milton's nephew, who was closely associated with Milton until the latter's death, and who had an unrivalled knowledge of his uncle's public and private life; that of John Aubrey, and that of the so-called anonymous biographer, whose identity is in dispute [21] but who writes from firsthand knowledge. It is to such sources, and not to Johnson or Wood, that we must go if we are to get anywhere near the truth about Milton's character. And the portrait of Milton that emerges from these early, and almost certainly reliable, accounts is far different from Johnson's portrait or Masson's. What Helen Darbishire has to say about the early *Lives* of Milton is particularly important. 'If they tell us little or nothing discreditable to Milton that is not simply because they were writing for edification. Perhaps there was little discreditable to tell. Aubrey was frankly unbiased and incurably indiscreet yet he has nothing worse to report than that Milton was whipped by his tutor at Cambridge and that he in turn whipped his nephews. And Wood, who was harshly disposed to Milton, gives evil interpretations but no evil facts.' [22] The picture that emerges from these contemporary biographies is, on the whole, quite an agreeable one: Milton is seen as a pleasant, interesting, sociable and likeable individual; above all he is *human*, quite unlike what Professor Wright calls 'the ogre originally created by his religious and political enemies, and revived by Dr Johnson a century later'. [23]

One of the early biographers did, however, supply two items of information about Milton which were the cause of a good deal of embarrassment to his later admirers. Edward Phillips tells us that Milton condemned two of his daughters 'to the performance of reading, and exactly pronouncing of all the languages of whatever book he should at one time or other think fit to peruse; *viz.* the Hebrew (and I think the Syriac), the Greek, the Latin, the Italian, Spanish, and French. All which sorts of books to be confined to read, without understanding one word must needs be a trial of patience almost beyond endurance; yet it was endured by both for a long time.' Another passage in Phillips was interpreted by Masson to mean that

Milton's *Doctrine and Discipline of Divorce* must have been written during his honeymoon. Jonathan Richardson, defending Milton against the charge of tyrannizing over his daughters relates that 'That Daughter . . . that was Thus Serviceable to her Excellent Father in his Distress, Express'd no Uneasiness that I ever heard of, when she gave accounts of Milton's Affairs to the Many Enquirers Lately; but on the Contrary, spoke of him with Great Tenderness; particularly I have been told She said He was Delightful Company, the Life of the Conversation, and That on Account of a Flow of Subject, and an Unaffected Chearfulness and Civility'. [24] Charles Williams has dealt rather harshly with the whole story which, he claimed, 'in its simple monstrosity, is quite inconceivable'. He dismisses it on two grounds: Milton would never have allowed his 'fastidious ear' to be offended by Deborah 'plunging through an uncomprehended vast of Virgil', and Deborah would never have been able to learn to read the Latin correctly, to say nothing of Hebrew, Greek, Italian, Spanish and French. Williams has his own explanation of Phillips's story. Milton needed someone to look up half-forgotten lines of poetry, and his daughter had to search for them among a mass of other lines, for the blind man will only be able to say *about* where the required line occurs. To the assistant, as Williams points out, it is a dull business: 'It is a much duller business if the desired reference is in a foreign language. . . . No wonder it seemed to Deborah Milton that she had read Virgil aloud to her father . . .' [25]

What Professor Wright called 'the final stroke in the denigration of Milton' was given by Masson, who accepted the traditional date for Milton's marriage, Whitsuntide 1643, and who pointed out that the *Doctrine and Discipline of Divorce* was published in July 1643. This is Masson's comment: 'That a man should have occupied himself on a Tract on Divorce ere his honeymoon was well over—should have written it perseveringly day after day within sound of his newly-wedded wife's footsteps and the very rustle of her dress on the stairs or in the neighbouring room—is a notion all but dreadful. And yet to some such notion, if Phillips's dating is correct, we seem to be shut up.' [26] But the researches of Helen Darbishire, Professor Wright and Burns Martin show beyond much doubt that Milton's first marriage took place not in 1643 but in 1642, the former date having been read into Edward Phillips's account by Toland. [27]

One other charge against Milton has for long exercised the minds of scholars: he has been accused of procuring the insertion into some editions of the *Eikon Basilike* of a supposititious prayer in order that he might attack it in his *Eikonoklastes*. The charge that Milton foisted this prayer was vigorously maintained by a Swedish scholar, S. B. Liljegren, in his *Studies in Milton* (1918), supported by Paul Morand, a French Miltonist, in his study of *The Effects of his Political Life on John Milton* (1939), and carefully considered by Professor Empson in a long Appendix to his book, *Milton's God* (revised edition, 1965). Empson's conclusion is that the story that Milton secured the insertion of the prayer 'is now above an even bet, rather more likely than not'. The contributions to the debate have grown so numerous, and the arguments so involved, that a reasonable discussion of the whole question would require a very large book.[28] Whether the story of the forgery is true or not, what are its implications for Milton's character? Scholars like R. W. Chambers thought it necessary to acquit Milton of the charge because, apparently, they believed that the imputation of forgery would do serious damage to the widely-held view that Milton was 'of lofty, large, and majestic mind'. But Professor Empson turned the tables on those who would use the conclusion that Milton was a forger to prove his wickedness by arguing that if we accept the story of the forgery and others like it as true, we end up with a more appealing portrait of Milton than the one Chambers was trying to perpetuate.

'Sad and funny though it is', Empson writes, 'for the de-nouncer of censorship to become a propaganda chief, Milton deserves respect . . . for rejecting brutal methods in favour of guile (not only here). So I don't feel that the action is too bad for Milton; he would think the divine purpose behind the Civil War justified propaganda tricks, and need not have thought this a particularly bad one. . . . The picture we get . . . of how Milton tackled his public duty makes him a broader and more adroit kind of man than is usually thought, less pedantic and self-enclosed, more humane, more capable of entering into other people's motives and sentiments . . . I think that to realize this improves *Paradise Lost*, in an underground way, because the chief reason why people interpret the poem as stupid and un-natural is that they believe the author was stupid and unnatural.'[29]

Many of his admirers have tried to show that Milton was more 'humane', less 'stupid and unnatural' than his detractors made him out to be, but few of them would have accepted Professor Empson's observations as good grounds for admiration. They did, however, provide other evidence to show that Milton actually possessed some appealing personal qualities, that he was generous, forgiving and endowed with a good deal of moral courage. Most people know him, as Helen Darbishire pointed out, as the harsh parent who forced his daughters to read to him in languages they did not understand; few people know him 'as the wronged but generous husband that took under his roof in a time of political danger not only his rebellious wife, but her parents and eight tiresome brothers and sisters'.[30] An important piece of evidence which throws favourable light on Milton's character is provided by the so-called anonymous biographer, who claimed that he felt no personal animosity towards the Royalists, 'but was forward to do any of them good Offices when their particular Cases afforded him ground to appear on their behalf. And especially, if on the score of Witt or Learning, they could lay claim to his peculiar Patronage. Of which there were instances, among others, the Grand child of the famous Spenser, a Papist suffering in his concerns in Ireland, and Sr. William Davenant when taken Prisoner, for both of whom he procur'd relief.'[31] We have evidence too that Milton was a capable and shrewd man of affairs: this is shown particularly in his dealings with his father-in-law Richard Powell, a subject investigated by J. M. French, whose conclusions are interesting: 'We see Milton', he writes, 'as a strict business man, frequently at law and successfully so . . . who knew how to manage his estate so as to reap a steady income despite depressions, wars and taxes. . . . Milton had a range of vision which included both God and the main chance.'[32]

Evidence of this kind makes it necessary to revise many old ideas about Milton's character. But there is one aspect of his character which even his most devoted admirers find extremely difficult, if not impossible, to defend: his deplorable manner of controversy. His prose works abound in harsh and unjust statements. Here is what he has to say about the Church of Andrewes, Herbert and Ferrar: 'Where was there a more ignorant, profane, and vicious clergy, learned in nothing but the antiquity of their pride, their covetousness, and superstition.' (*Eikonoklastes*, Bohn 1, 382.) Bishops, he writes, 'after a shameful end in this life (which God grant them) shall be thrown down eternally into the darkest and deepest gulf of hell'. (*Of Reformation*,

Bohn II, 419). One thing can, however, be urged in Milton's defence: he was moved, as Douglas Bush pointed out, 'as bookish idealists—and Church Fathers—often have been, by a genuinely impersonal fury against the enemies of a sacred cause'. In the prose works, his anger is often directed against personifications rather than persons. What E. H. Visiak writes about his treatment of Pius V is very apt: 'Whether he was aware in composing *In Quintum Novembris* that Pius V, whom he therein represents as a licentious miscreant, was, in fact, a man of unexceptionable life and exemplary morals is doubtful, but would not have signified from his point of view, which was passionately propagandist. For him this particular Pope was *any* Pope.'[33]

Many of those who helped to revise traditional notions about Milton's character also played a part in the even more important movement dedicated to the rescue of Milton's thought from the almost universal disesteem into which it had fallen in the nineteenth century. In showing the worth and range of Milton's ideas, these critics made the whole nineteenth-century approach to his thought seem inadequate. The significance of the work of Saurat, Tillyard, Hanford, Bush, Grierson and the many other scholars and critics who stressed the value of Milton's thought becomes apparent only when considered against the background of nineteenth-century criticism. It may seem rash to generalize about a century of literary criticism: it is, however, safe to say that from 1800 to about 1915, Milton's ideas, if discussed at all, were treated either with distaste or indifference. Shelley regarded *Paradise Lost* as a monument to decaying superstition; Keats believed that the philosophy of the epic, and, indeed, of the other works, might be 'tolerably understood by one not much advanced in years'; Leigh Hunt drew attention to Milton's ideas only to express the belief that they detracted from the interest of his work; Bagehot emphasized the poverty of Milton's thought; Macaulay and Emerson ignored it, and Landor, who declared himself averse 'to everything relating to theology', expressed his dislike for it. Lowell and Stephen, James Thorpe points out, found Milton's philosophy worthless, 'Birrell could discover nothing but a story, and Saintsbury avowed that Milton's ideas did not merit discussion'.[34] Matthew Arnold had little respect for Milton the thinker: as a great artist 'in the great style' he considered him unsurpassed by any other English poet. Thorpe suggests that even the most favourable Victorian attitude can be reduced to a simple syllogism: Milton's theology (reality to him) is worthless; Milton's stock of ideas is only theology; Milton's ideas are worthless.

The nineteenth-century idea that it was unrewarding to pay much attention to Milton's thought found its final and classic expression in Raleigh's verdict that *Paradise Lost* 'is not the less an eternal monument because it is a monument to dead ideas'.[35] Like other critics in the nineteenth-century tradition, Raleigh virtually restricted the value of the epic to its style: the modern reader, he believed, could not be expected to accommodate his mind to the 'anthropomorphic theology' of the poem. Young people, he suggested, who read poetry for 'sonorous suggestions' and 'processions of vague shapes', may love Milton: adults, who read it for 'its matter and sentiment', find little to interest them in Milton, and seldom return to him. The implications of nineteenth-century praise and blame were clear to most critics of the twentieth century. Waldock pointed out that if such praise and blame were just, if Raleigh's *Paradise Lost* was the real *Paradise Lost*, it would be difficult to predict for the epic 'any lasting future except as a majestic derelict, a great white elephant of poetry without real use or function'.[36] The poem, as interpreted by nineteenth-century critics, has no real chance of speaking to the modern world.

On the issue of the value and relevance of Milton's ideas, the twentieth-century critics of his work divided into two groups. One group, which included most of the critics who most strongly defended Milton's style and language, found Raleigh's reading of the epic unacceptable, and set out to show that nineteenth-century patronage of *Paradise Lost* for its grandeur of style and insufficiency of thought had been misplaced, and that there was no need to base Milton's reputation solely on the early books of the epic and on the grandeur of Satan. On the other hand, many of those who found serious fault with the style and language of the epic tended to accept the nineteenth-century verdict on Milton's ideas. Eliot could not accept with any enthusiasm the views of Addison and Johnson that *Paradise Lost* would always be acceptable because of its theme; instead, he suggested in his second essay on Milton, if a modern lover of poetry could read the epic with absorbed attention, this would be on account of 'the extraordinary style which because of its perpetual variety compels us to curiosity to know what is coming next', rather than because of the subject matter. Waldock approached *Paradise Lost* in the belief that 'it stands or falls, as every work of literature ultimately must, by the sense it makes', found that in many places it did not make sense to him. His final verdict on the significance of the poem resembles Eliot's: he believed that we shall go on reading the poem for ever, 'for the glory of the writing and for the spirit of Milton that so lives in whatever he wrote'. Leavis dismissed Milton's thought with the words: 'The Miltonic mind has nothing to offer that could justify obscurity.'[37]

J. H. Hanford, writing in 1919, when the movement to shift some of the attention from Milton's style to his ideas was just beginning, described the situation which prevailed at that time. For most readers, he pointed out, the nineteenth-century estimate of the poet's thought, embodied in Raleigh's *Milton*, was the final one: *Paradise Lost*, if read at all, was read 'for its art, its eloquence, its elevation'.[38] Two years before Hanford wrote this, Edwin Greenlaw made one of the first modern attempts to break through the barriers of 'style' and 'art' and to make readers see in *Paradise Lost* something more than what Keats called 'a beautiful and grand curiosity'. Greenlaw expressed his concern about the fate of the epic in critical history: like Spenser's *Faerie Queene* it had come to be patronized for its insufficiency of thought. Like Spenser, Milton had been praised for 'poetic' qualities at the expense of intellectual ability. Greenlaw was anxious to show that there was really no need to limit the significance of *Paradise Lost* to its purely 'poetic' qualities, that Milton's thought deserved more consideration than it had hitherto received. It is interesting to note that Greenlaw did not try to show that Milton's theology was of living interest; and he did not ask 'unbelieving' readers to suspend their disbelief. Instead, he proposed a reinterpretation and revaluation of the poem in terms of humanism, avoiding Raleigh's conclusion that Milton's 'Puritan' theology had turned the epic into 'a chapel of ease for his own mind' by arguing that the philosophy of *Paradise Lost* derived ultimately not from the Book of Genesis but from Greece. 'The story of the fall of Adam', he suggested, 'immediately gains significance and interest if we recognize that the apple is but a symbol, and that Milton's real theme is to show how Adam fell because he did not stand the test of temperance.'[39] Hanford, who belonged, like Greenlaw, to the school of criticism which stressed the importance of Milton's thought, also avoided a theological interpretation of the ideas in the epic, believing that the 'humanistic' approach pursued by Greenlaw was bound to lead to a higher valuation of Milton's 'original contribution as a humane and philosophical thinker'. He was prepared to admit that Milton had expressed his thought in a terminology which had become obsolete, but this need not, he believed, alienate the modern mind: Milton's 'obsolete theology' could be converted, without undue difficulty, into modern terms. To refit *Paradise Lost* for the modern world Hanford found it necessary to emphasize the power of Milton's 'poetic and philosophic thought' at the expense of 'the dogmatic aspects of his inherited theology'. As a result of the work of the scholars who belonged to the new movement, Milton began to emerge as a Renaissance artist. The old Puritan image was considerably modified: in Smart's words the aim was to get Milton 'completely and resolutely demassonized'. Some scholars went to considerable lengths to show that the traditional image of Milton as a solemn, staid and narrow-minded Puritan was false. Liljegren, for example, painted a portrait which made him look less like a seventeenth-century Puritan than a ruthlessly Machiavellian Renaissance man, who was not above lying and forgery when these suited his ends. On the intellectual level, he began to be seen as an independent thinker, the student of occult and heterodox books.[40] The speculations and discoveries of the participants in the new movement led to a pronounced change of attitude towards *Paradise Lost*, which was gradually transformed from a monument to dead ideas into what Rajan called 'a mine of occult speculation, materialist heresies and Kantian absolutes'.

In this transformation Denis Saurat played a leading part. In spite of the fact that most of what he wrote about Milton's thought has been either drastically revised or completely contradicted by later scholars, the very fact that he focused attention on Milton's ideas made his work extremely valuable. As C. S. Lewis pointed out in his *Preface to Paradise Lost*, it is to Saurat that most of the credit must go for having rescued Milton criticism 'from the drowsy praise of his organ music and babble about the majestic rolls of proper names'. Like Hanford and Greenlaw, he adopted a 'non-theological' approach to Milton's work. Believing that there was in the poetry 'a philosophical interest susceptible of universal appeal', he felt that in order to make this interest clear it was necessary to ignore the theology of the epic, 'to disentangle from the theological rubbish the permanent and human interest' of Milton's thought. He sought to divorce Milton as completely as possible from seventeenth-century Protestantism: in Saurat's synthesis Milton's God is, as he puts it, 'far from the God of popular belief or even orthodox theology. He is, properly speaking, identical with the Absolute of nineteenth-century philosophy. He is no Creator external to His Creation, but Total and Perfect Being which includes in Himself the whole of Space and the whole of Time.' He found the following passage in *Paradise Lost* particularly significant:

> Boundless the Deep, because I am who fill
> Infinitude, nor vacuous the space.
> Though I uncircumscribed myself retire,
> And put not forth my goodness, which is free
> To act or not, Necessity and Chance
> Approach not mee, and what I will is Fate.
>
> VII. 170

This passage was important to Saurat because he believed it showed Milton's indebtedness to the *Zohar*, a thirteenth-century compendium of all the non-orthodox Jewish traditions, thus illustrating the range and daring of Milton's speculations. It also seemed to illustrate Milton's mastery of ideas: 'Pantheism, materialism, doctrines of free will and of fate as God's will—by a truly remarkable *tour de force* Milton has logically tied those four somewhat antagonistic conceptions into one solid knot; he has done it in six lines. . . .'[41] As Saurat presents him, Milton, instead of being 'an isolated thinker lost in seventeenth-century England', becomes 'the brilliant representative of an antique and complex tradition'. Saurat's investigations induced a new respect for Milton's thought, and made it no longer safe to dismiss his ideas as naive and entirely conventional. Saurat revered him as 'the marvellous poet, the profound thinker'.

Suarat's picture of the profound thinker is pretty well authenticated in Basil Willey's *Seventeenth-Century Background*, where the formidable problems which faced Milton in the composition of *Paradise Lost* are brilliantly analysed. To read Willey's analysis of the problems which Milton had to face and resolve is to realize that his performance, quite apart from the Grand Style, the epic similes and the characterization of Satan, entitles him to respectful consideration as a man of profound and remarkable intellectual power. Willey's study makes it clear that Milton was extremely subtle and ingenious in the ordering of his epic material. He had to be, faced as he was with problems like that suggested by Willey in the following: 'Milton, believing . . . in

"Knowledge", and in "Reason" as the choice of good by a free agent cognisant of evil, selects as the subject of his greatest poem a fable which represents the acquisition of these very things as the source of all our woe.'[42]

To almost all Milton critics the 'New Movement' represented a salutary force: Saurat in particular stimulated a new interest in Milton's sources and in the ideas underlying the epic. But many critics who were in sympathy with the aims of the 'New Movement' had serious reservations about the fundamentally non-theological approach of critics like Saurat. C. S. Lewis, for example, was particularly disturbed by Saurat's desire 'to disentangle from the theological rubbish the permanent and human interest' of Milton's thought. To this Lewis replied quite simply in his *Preface to Paradise Lost* that Milton's thought, when purged of its theology, did not exist. Critics like Lewis, Bush, Williams, Rosemond Tuve and Tillyard considered the theological approach to Milton's ideas essential to a proper interpretation of the epic. Believing as they did that Milton had chosen to make his poem inescapably theological, they also believed that the refusal to take Milton's theology seriously, and the attempts to avoid discussing it in dealing with *Paradise Lost*, amounted to a refusal to take the real theme of the epic seriously. This refusal meant remaking the poem, and behind the attitude of those who advocated the 'theological' approach was the view that it is impossible to 'remake' the subject of a poem without deviating from the poet's own intentions, and without reading its significance in aspects which the poet never intended to make predominant. To the 'theological' critics, the readings of the 'New Movement' were at worst distortions, and at best evasions, rather like Professor Empson's famous interpretation of Herbert's *Sacrifice*.[43]

Many of the critics of the 'New Movement' seemed, in effect, to acquiesce in Raleigh's verdict that Milton's epic, if read as a poem with a theological subject, is a monument to dead ideas, having little chance of speaking to the modern world. But Raleigh's view that Milton's ideas were 'dead' was based on his belief that 'the epic poem, which in its natural form is a kind of cathedral for the ideas of a nation, is by him transformed into a chapel-of-ease for his own mind, a monument to his own genius and his own habits of thought'.[44] Raleigh obviously regarded *Paradise Lost* as a predominantly Puritan poem, a vehicle for Milton's own unorthodox religious beliefs—beliefs which, being peculiar to Milton, could never enjoy any wide acceptance or sympathy, and which consequently took from the universality of his poem. For Raleigh, Milton's thought was primarily theological, the theology of the epic was Puritan, and consequently the ideas in the poem could have little modern relevance. Hence his emphasis—and that of the nineteenth century—on the style as the saving virtue of *Paradise Lost*. In the light of Raleigh's views, the anxiety of the 'New Movement' to get away from theological interpretations of the poem, to divorce Milton from seventeenth-century Protestantism and to make him look like a daring Renaissance thinker, is understandable. To admit the theological subject seemed, to critics of the 'New Movement', to concede that *Paradise Lost* was a 'Puritan' poem and thus a monument to dead ideas.

But the most important aspect of the work of the 'theological' critics was their effort to show that such a concession was altogether unnecessary, and that Raleigh's view of the theology of the epic as predominantly unorthodox and 'Puritan' was false. By emphasizing the predominantly 'Catholic' quality of the poem, by showing that Milton had dealt with the great universal truths, and by pointing out that Raleigh, Saurat and many others had—with the heterodox *De Doctrina* too much in mind—seriously exaggerated the nature and extent of Milton's obtrusion of personal heresies into the epic, these critics did much to show that Milton's theology, far from narrowing the scope and relevance of the poem, tended to give it just that universality which Saurat and others had been seeking outside the 'theological rubbish'. Modern scholarship has established beyond much doubt that Milton was quite conscious of the dangers of making an epic poem—as Raleigh suggested he did—into a chapel-of-ease for his own mind. He realized as well as any of his critics did that a successful epic poem 'is the property not of a person but of an epoch. It could never be "doctrinal to a nation" . . . if it were concerned . . . with the special and individual convictions of its author. If it is to appeal at all to the reader's sensibility, it can only do so on conditions which every reader accepts.'[45]

Perhaps the most important single modern contribution to the study of Milton's thought is Maurice Kelley's *This Great Argument*. Its appearance in 1941 solved many problems and ended many arguments. Kelley's study of Milton's theology makes it quite clear that there is no difference in dogma between

Paradise Lost and *De Doctrina Christiana*, and that the latter is the one document indispensable to the study of the religious beliefs set forth in the epic. Kelley pointed out that many previous scholars—he referred to the 'New Movement' in particular—had followed false trails in their search for the sources of Milton's epic, and had 'set forth patently inaccurate expositions' of the nature of Milton's thought. The reason for this was that critics like Saurat had failed to pay sufficient attention to the close relationship between the treatise and the epic. Kelley's study showed that 'Saurat's identification of Milton's concept of God with the Absolute of nineteenth-century philosophy is not tenable'; he could not accept Saurat's idea that *Paradise Lost* presents a theory of creation by retraction; and he refuted Saurat's argument that Milton was a consistent and logical philosopher by showing that he was 'capable of maintaining, and sometimes did pursue, incompatible trends of thought when his individual views conflicted with a more generally accepted doctrine'.[46] Even before Kelley's establishment of the intimate doctrinal relationship between *Paradise Lost* and *De Doctrina*, other scholars had made it clear that the *Zohar* did not provide the proper perspective for the study of the main ideas underlying *Paradise Lost*: Harris Fletcher pointed out that it is most unlikely that Milton even knew of the *Zohar*, although the 'jealousy motive' employed in Book ix of *Paradise Lost* may well have been borrowed from another rabbinical source, a work on Jewish history which usually passes under the name of Yosippon, and which was readily accessible to seventeenth-century readers.[47]

The discovery that *De Doctrina Christiana* and the epic are identical from the point of view of religious dogma, and that certain important portions of *Paradise Lost* are poetic restatements of beliefs already expressed in the prose treatise invalidated much of the work of critics of the 'New Movement'. 'Behind *Paradise Lost* and its high argument', Kelley emphasized, is an aetiological explanation of the problem of evil, which is Christian, Protestant, and seventeenth century to the core.'[48] This puts Kabbalistic and Renaissance interpretations firmly in their place: the trouble is that it also seems to lend authority to Raleigh's view of the epic as a monument to dead ideas. For *De Doctrina Christiana* is an extremely heterodox document, a work to which Raleigh's description of *Paradise Lost*—'a chapel-of-ease for his own mind, a monument to his own genius and habits of thought'—might well be applied. Surely then, if we accept Kelley's verdict that the treatise and the epic are doctrinally identical, we cannot avoid applying Raleigh's verdict to the epic also, and agreeing that a poem setting forth a highly personal interpretation of the doctrines of seventeenth-century Protestantism can have little interest or relevance for twentieth-century readers, even when such readers are Christians.

There is, as has already been suggested, an answer to this difficulty. The answer lies in the fact that although the unorthodoxies present in *De Doctrina* can also be detected in *Paradise Lost*, there is a vast difference between the treatise and the epic in the presentation of Milton's heterodox theology. Rajan stressed the essential difference between the two when he pointed out that 'Milton seems to go out of his way to avoid harassing the reader of *Paradise Lost* with his personal beliefs, and in the effort to do so he tones down his heresies as much as he can without becoming dishonest.'[49] A central point in the theological system expounded in *De Doctrina* is the absolute inferiority of the Son to the Father, which Milton tries to demonstrate by referring to the Scriptures, whereas in *Paradise Lost*, although a skilled theologian may detect Arianism, it is not explicitly set forth as it is in the treatise. In places, even, Milton seems to go out of his way to allay any suspicions of heresy which his readers might have formed. In Book III, for example, we find this reference to the Son:

> Because thou hast, though thron'd in highest bliss
> Equal to God and equally enjoying
> God-like fruition, quitted all to save
> A world from utter loss . . .
>
> III. 305–308

When the contents and the existence of *De Doctrina* were unknown, generations of orthodox and theologically conscious readers failed to detect heresy in *Paradise Lost*; until 1825, when the treatise was published, Milton was regarded as 'a poet impeccably sound of faith'. Bishop Newton declared that he was generally 'truly orthodox'; Trapp, in his Preface to the Latin edition of *Paradise Lost* wrote of the poem: 'omne ex parte orthodoxum'; Dr Johnson, who, as Sewell pointed out, 'would not easily acquit Milton of heterodoxy', declared that Milton was 'untainted by any heretical peculiarity of opinion'. Tillyard drew attention to the fact that for a century and a half the epic was considered sufficiently orthodox to be set up as an example by orthodox divines of the eighteenth and nineteenth centuries. Thorpe reminds us that in the eighteenth century Milton's poem was venerated as one of the principal supports of orthodox' Christianity. Rajan, who accepted Kelley's conclusions about the doctrinal similarities between the epic and the treatise, suggested that if we collate *Paradise Lost* with the *De Doctrina* it is Arian. 'But', he argued, 'read it as it was meant to be read, by itself, as an epic poem, not a systematic theology, and the heresy fades in a background of incantation. The scriptural reminiscences reverberate orthodoxy.'[50]

In view of such evidence, C. S. Lewis, whose own point of view was one of sophisticated orthodoxy, was justified in claiming that *Paradise Lost* is 'Catholic in the sense of basing its poetry on conceptions that have been held "always and everywhere and by all". This Catholic quality is so predominant that it is the first impression any unbiased reader would receive. Heretical elements exist in it, but are only discoverable by search: any criticism which forces them into the foreground is mistaken.' Lewis summed up his own views on the religious ideas of the epic by saying that 'as far as doctrine goes, the poem is overwhelmingly Christian. Except for a few isolated passages it is not even specifically Protestant or Puritan. It gives the great central tradition . . . its invitation to join in this great ritual *mimesis* of the Fall is one which all Christendom in all lands or ages can accept.'[51] This conclusion, supported as it is by a great volume of evidence, marks an important advance on the nineteenth-century approach, which made it seem undesirable to take the theological theme seriously, because the theology of the epic was equated with sectarianism. The adjustment of the nineteenth-century view of *Paradise Lost* as a 'Puritan' epic, and the modern tendency to see it as an essentially 'Catholic' work make it necessary to qualify Raleigh's view of it as 'a monument to dead ideas' by saying that it will be such a monument only when Christianity itself—and not merely seventeenth-century Protestantism as seen through nineteenth-century eyes—has become obsolete.

CHAPTER SIX

Modern Relevance

Even if we agree that *Paradise Lost* is sufficiently Catholic or universal to be readily accessible to all kinds of Christians, there still remains the problem, often hinted at in modern criticism of the poem, that many potential readers are not Christians at all. By stressing the essential orthodoxy of its ideas the 'theological' critics may have extended the relevance of *Paradise Lost* to Christians of all kinds. But their repeated insistence on the theological theme as the real one tends to confine the appeal of the poem to readers who share Christian beliefs, and to repel the non-Christian reader. Worse still, the traditional and 'orthodox' Christian theology of *Paradise Lost* seems to repel even some Christian writers: Eliot, for example, in his 1936 essay on Milton, found the theology of the epic 'repellent', and thought the mythology would better have been left in the Book of Genesis. Professor Empson explained the attitude of such 'civilized Christians' as Eliot. He agreed with C. S. Lewis that Milton's God is, after all, merely the traditional God of Christianity. But, he explained, Eliot presumably felt, 'as many modern Christians do, that he wished people wouldn't mention these nasty old myths'.[1] If even modern Christians like Eliot find Christian mythology unattractive, as Empson claims they do, what chance has a poem like *Paradise Lost*, based as it is firmly and unequivocally on traditional Christian beliefs, of appealing to those who are either indifferent or hostile to Christianity? In modern discussion of the poem, this question constantly recurs. More often than not, it is intended merely as a rhetorical question. What, for instance, is a modern unbeliever to make of Adam's statement that he will 'to the hand of Heav'n submit, However chastning' (XI. 373)? J. B. Broadbent suggested that such a sentiment is felt as 'a betrayal . . . alternatively, as unconscious doublethink'.[2] Milton's reliance on the major doctrines of Christianity, as Broadbent points out, makes the poem subject to all the criticisms of orthodoxy 'from Montaigne through Blake to Kathleen Nott'. Such criticisms tend to present Christian mythology as 'crude and inadequate'. Empson would go even further. 'What Christians are worshipping', he argues, 'with their incessant advertisements for torture, is literally the Devil.'[3] In the eighteenth century, the epic was revered as one of the main supports of orthodox religion: in the twentieth, many people dislike it for this very reason.

Milton himself was conscious of the fact that the nature of his theme tended to limit the appeal of his poem. In Book VII we have the Invocation:

> Still govern thou my song
> Urania, and fit audience find, though few.

And in 1674 Marvell, in a poem prefixed to the second edition of *Paradise Lost*, expressed a view of the poem which was to find an echo in much later criticism. Marvell wrote:

> That Majesty which through thy Work doth Reign
> Draws the Devout, deterring the Profane.

It is almost a commonplace in twentieth-century Milton criticism that not all readers, whatever their erudition, can derive full satisfaction from Milton's religious poetry. Christian humanists like C. S. Lewis, Douglas Bush and Sir Herbert Grierson must, as R. M. Adams puts it, 'necessarily experience Milton's poetry in a specially rich and intimate way'.[4] But modern critics place strong emphasis on the theological barrier which stands between modern readers—apart from the Christian humanists—and the full enjoyment of a poem like *Paradise Lost*. At present the epic occupies a singular and rather unenviable position in literary criticism. This is due mainly to two things. It is, Lord David Cecil to the contrary notwithstanding, the greatest Christian poem in English; it is also the greatest non-dramatic long poem in the language. There is a further consideration, not quite so important as the other two, but nevertheless deserving of attention in any discussion of Milton's appeal to the present age: Milton's frequent use of classical mythology throughout the poem.

This, we are frequently reminded with reference to *Paradise Lost*, is a post-Christian age. Although Professor Empson feels it necessary to deplore the rise of a 'neo-Christian movement', associated in some way or other with T. S. Eliot, there is no mistaking or denying the general trend. Most of those who, in England at any rate, devote themselves to literary criticism seem to share the feeling expressed by D. H. Lawrence in 1924 that 'the Christian venture is done'. In such a climate of opinion, it is not surprising that critics tend to emphasize the indifference which Milton's theological ideas are likely to encounter from the modern reader. The post-Christian, seeking to cultivate his sense of spiritual health, will hardly turn to Milton; instead, he will probably have recourse to writers like Yeats and Lawrence, who have made major attempts to find satisfaction outside Christianity for man's religious impulse. Critics are at pains to point out that in *Paradise Lost* Milton has little to say that can interest us. Once upon a time the poem seemed to deal with the greatest of all subjects: today, we are told, the Fall of Man is a subject no longer operating within the general imagination. C. Day Lewis believes that for modern man 'the story of Adam and Eve is an old wives' tale—or a stockbroker's joke'. Lionel Trilling feels that our modern literary feeling inclines us to admire Milton only if we believe with Blake that he was of the Devil's party; and, he suggests, 'the paradox of the *felix culpa* . . . appeals to us for other than theological reasons and serves to validate all sins and falls, which we take to be the signs of life'. George Watson's impression is that 'for better or worse, most twentieth-century readers are simply not curious to know the answer to the questions that Milton poses in his greatest poem'. Such comments as these do not record purely personal impressions; the views they express are representative.[5]

Apart from the general feeling of hostility or indifference to Milton's theology, it is possible to suggest other reasons why critics feel that this is Milton's period 'out'. One reason is simply the length of his greatest poem. The reason for a great deal of the modern neglect of Milton, according to John Wain, is 'an honourable one to Milton. . . . It is simply that one of his chief virtues has come to be regarded as a vice. Milton has an extraordinary power of sustaining large structures. . . . But this is exactly what the modern reader does not want him to do. The modern ear is attuned entirely to short, concentrated poems.'[6] Modern literary feeling has been conditioned very largely by Symbolist doctrines. And one of the chief tenets of the Symbolist movement is that long poems are impossible. If a modern poet does want to write a long poem, Wain points out, he will not write it like *Paradise Lost*: instead, he will adopt a discontinuous method. The result will be 'cinematic poetry' like *The Waste Land* or Pound's *Cantos*. Milton's theology, the length of the epic, and the fact that the modern reader can no longer be counted upon to respond imaginatively to the wealth of classical allusion in his poetry, seem to make the position of *Paradise Lost* extremely precarious. Most critics would seem to feel, at any rate, that full participation in *Paradise Lost* is now virtually impossible; some would even go so far as to suggest that it is more remote from us than Homer's *Iliad*, and that by comparison Shakespeare is thoroughly contemporary. It would, of course, be a mistake to suggest that such an attitude is peculiar to the middle of the twentieth century. Even in 1900 Sir Walter Raleigh was claiming that 'the drifting away of the popular belief from the tenets of Milton's theology doubtless does something to explain the lukewarm interest taken by most educated English readers in *Paradise Lost*'.[7] And in 1859, Bagehot, on behalf of his own 'irreverent generation', concurred with Dr Johnson's sentiment that nobody wished the epic any longer than it is; some, he suggested, wished it shorter.

Some earlier critics found it possible to circumvent the theological difficulties presented by the epic. Shelley, for example, was able to admire the subject matter of the poem, in spite of his declared aversion for theology, by looking upon it as a violation of the popular creed, and claiming that it 'contains within itself a philosophical refutation of that system of which, by a strange and natural antithesis, it has been the chief popular support' (*A Defence of Poetry*). Blake also inverted Milton's declared intentions; in his famous epigram he described Milton as 'a true Poet and of the Devil's party without knowing it'.[8] There are several modern critics who are conscious of the difficulties presented by Milton's theological ideas to non-Christian readers, and who are also anxious that *Paradise Lost* should be enjoyed as fully as possible even by those who do not share Christian beliefs. These critics have not, however, gone as far as Shelley and Blake did in refitting the poem for the modern mind. Instead, they have made tentative suggestions for a completely non-theological reading, a reading which would fit it into the framework of modern thought, and thus give it some positive significance, apart from its style and language, for modern readers devoid of Christian sensibility. If the celestial cycle is no longer operating within the general imagination, no longer capable of stirring the minds of readers of poetry, then perhaps it is possible to reinterpret the poem in terms of ideas and beliefs which are more immediately relevant to modern modes of thought.

Milton, F. T. Prince suggests, constantly points in the direction of allegory; the modern reader to whom the claim to religious assent may be an obstacle, can try to 'get round it' by 'allegorizing or psychologizing' what Milton gives us. Such an approach, applied to the last two Books of the epic, might, according to Prince, recall Proust's dictum that '*les vrais Paradis sont toujours les Paradis qui sont perdus*'; or the conclusion of the poem 'might be held to crystallize something which is inherent in man's experience of time, his feeling for past, present and future'. Finally, perhaps, the expulsion from Paradise, together with the preceding view of world history, might be seen as a vehicle for Blake's 'two contrary states of the human soul', innocence and experience.[9] Like Prince, Bernard Bergonzi suggested a reading of the epic that might evade the theological difficulty. If we look upon Book IV, which deals with the enjoyment of Eden, and Book IX, which describes its loss, as 'the imaginative centre of the poem', then its meaning, as Bergonzi sees it, may have a good deal to do with the Freudian 'birth trauma', the expulsion from the womb 'into a world where life and death are inextricably mixed'.[10]

There can be no doubt that such suggestions point to extremely interesting, indeed fascinating, possibilities. Critics who make them, however, leave themselves open to charges of distorting or evading the real theme. Such a charge, at any rate, cannot be brought against Professor J. H. Summers, who has been able to demonstrate the modern relevance of one aspect of Milton's thought in *Paradise Lost* without having recourse to allegory. Taking as his text the line from Book VIII, 'Which two great Sexes animate the World' (l. 151), Summers discusses Milton's treatment of sex, and suggests, with justification, that 'anyone who reads *Paradise Lost* carefully today is almost inevitably reminded of William Blake and D. H. Lawrence'. Lawrence, he points out,[11] 'was sexually a puritan in something of the sense that Milton was: he attacked the false and the fashionable, not because he believed sex low, but because he believed it central and noble and capable of a kind of perfection'. Milton's affinity with Lawrence is clear in his celebration of the love of Adam and Eve before the Fall:

> Whatever Hypocrites austerely talk
> Of purity and place and innocence,
> Defaming as impure what God declares
> Pure, and commands to some, leaves free to all . . .
>
> IV. 744–747

It is also clear in his rejection of everything that debases real love:

> . . . the bought smile
> Of Harlots, loveless, joyless, unindear'd,
> Casual fruition . . .

IV. 765–767

Many critics found the attempts to overcome the theological challenge by allegorizing or psychologizing what Milton gives us quite unacceptable. They argued that a wholesale evasion of the theological approach could only lead to a restricted and distorted reading of the epic whose theme, they insisted, was predominantly theological. It is all very well to read symbolic meanings into the works of writers who deliberately employ symbolic language: to do so in Milton's case, at least on a large scale, is almost necessarily to misread him. It may well be true, many of these critics agreed, that the religious doctrines out of which Milton built his major poems are no longer in fashion today, but to avoid misreading him utterly, they argued, the modern reader must try to understand Milton's religious outlook and try to cultivate at least a temporary sympathy for the beliefs underlying his poetry. This brings us face to face with the conflict between the 'historical' and the 'non-historical' approaches, a conflict which is at the very heart of the Milton Controversy. On one side we have those who insist that to read Milton aright we must think in terms of seventeenth-century theology and refrain from introducing our own modern conventions and habits of thought into Milton's world. On the other we have those who believe that it is not possible—and even if it were, not desirable—to refrain from using our own modern insights, although as a result *Paradise Lost* may acquire new colours and meanings which Milton never dreamt of.

Douglas Bush represented an extreme reaction from the modern critical attempts to adapt *Paradise Lost* to modern taste. The critics who suggested Freudian and Proustian interpretations tended to reform the poem along modern lines: Bush suggested that instead the modern world might do well to reform its taste along Miltonic lines. He quoted Wordsworth's lines with approval:

> We must be free or die, who speak the tongue
> That Shakespeare spake; the faith and morals hold
> Which Milton held.

He saw in Milton's poetry a powerful means of correcting and reforming our age: 'We need the shock of encountering a poet to whom good and evil are distinct realities, a poet . . . who sees in human life an eternal contest between irreligious pride and religious humility.'[12] Whatever one may think about the validity of this attitude, its usefulness may justifiably be questioned. The modern world may well be as unregenerate as Bush claims it is, but Milton's poetry is hardly likely to emerge with enhanced literary prestige if it is used as a prophylactic against religious and moral decline.

Is there, however, a danger of exaggerating, perhaps seriously, the extent to which *Paradise Lost* is out of touch with modern taste, or at least the extent to which full participation in the epic is difficult for modern readers? Has the knowledge of the Christian-classical background from which Milton's ideas derive really become so limited, even among educated readers, as to be almost non-existent? Whatever is thought about the modern decline of classical studies and the widespread rejection of Christian belief, it seems rather difficult to accept the suggestion that Christian sensibility, as distinct from Christian belief, has no longer any real meaning for educated modern readers. After all, as Bernard Bergonzi pointed out, Christian sensibility has been 'an informing principle in over a thousand years of Western literature'. Surely, even in the thought of our 'post-Christian' age, the Christian heritage still retains some of its old influence: the Christian story has not vanished entirely from the modern consciousness.

E. M. W. Tillyard made an interesting case for the modern relevance of most of the main ideas underlying *Paradise Lost*. He pointed to 'certain fundamental and simple ideas which, founded on his experience, dominated Milton's mind, and which, to some extent, were symbolized by his theology'. He argued that these ideas 'are of more than temporary relevance, and they constitute a permanently credible attitude to life'. Many of the basic ideas of the epic, he thought, had nothing specifically to do with the seventeenth century: their appeal was independent of changing fashions and modes of belief. They found their way, as Housman put it, to 'something in man which is obscure and latent, something older than the present organization of his nature'. Considering Milton's work in the light of Maud Bodkin's *Archetypal Patterns in Poetry*, Tillyard believed that Milton was close to primitive and elemental habits of mind.

Miss Bodkin, he pointed out, finds Milton rich in the expression of 'archetypal patterns', myths or symbols which are 'rooted in primitive life', and which have the power 'to evoke a particularly keen response from the human mind'.[13] Jung, as well as Blake, Lawrence, Freud and Proust, can thus be invoked with a real sense of relevance in modern discussion of Milton's poetry.

It is well to remember that not all of *Paradise Lost* demands on the part of the reader an acquaintance with classical literature or Christian myth. Many passages can be enjoyed without background knowledge: such passages are to be found in all twelve Books. A reading of such passages, it is sometimes suggested, ought to provide a good introduction to the poem. John Wain wrote that if he wished to convert a modern reader to the view that Milton was a great poet he would begin by showing him the quotations from Milton's work in *The Oxford Dictionary of Quotations*. 'If one could get it into his head', Wain believed, 'that Milton's long poems, far from being merely unreadable, were a quarry in which one could pick up such jewels as these, he might turn to them.'[14]

But it might be argued that the criticism of *Paradise Lost* which has been based on outright hostility to the beliefs embodied in the poem, and that which has tried to fabricate an adulterated version to accommodate the reader who does not like theology, are both fundamentally wrong-headed. It is hardly the essential business of a literary critic to concern himself with the truth or untruth, the popularity or unpopularity, of Milton's religious beliefs, or to stress his value as a moral guide. The kind of question with which the literary critic should more certainly concern himself when dealing with a poem like *Paradise Lost* is, in Cormican's words, 'the extent to which theology and morality are transmuted into poetry'.[15] In *The Sacred Wood*, T. S. Eliot wrote that if he asked himself why he preferred the poetry of Dante to that of Shakespeare, his answer would have to be that it seemed to illustrate 'a saner attitude towards the mystery of life'. But commenting on this preference, and on others like it, Eliot remarked that in such questions we appear to be leaving the domain of criticism of 'poetry'.

This comment might be applied quite aptly to a great deal of Milton criticism. Many of Milton's apologists have expressed a liking for his ideas, and many of those who have questioned his eminence have shown a distaste for them, without seriously pausing to consider whether these ideas, attractive or repellent, have been turned into poetry. Douglas Bush's view of Milton as a writer whose ideas are 'very close to what many modern thinkers have been declaring are necessary to our own necessary regeneration', has little to do with Milton's value as a poet, and far more to do with ethical than with literary criticism. On the other hand, Pound's censure of Milton and Virgil because 'they muck about with a moral' would be justified only if he could show that these poets had failed to turn the moral into poetry. Eliot, dealing with Dante, advocated an approach to the work of that poet which, if adopted in Milton's case, would lead to more fruitful and relevant criticism of *Paradise Lost*. 'We must', Eliot suggested, 'show first in a particular case—our case is Dante—that the philosophy is essential to the structure and that the structure is essential to the poetic beauty of the parts; and we must show that the philosophy is employed in a different form from that which it takes in admittedly unsuccessful philosophical poems.'[16]

It is useful to consider the modern view that the ideas embodied in Milton's epic make it virtually unacceptable to most readers, in the light of Eliot's views on Shakespeare and Dante, expressed in his essay, *Shakespeare and the Stoicism of Seneca*. 'In truth', he claimed, 'neither Shakespeare nor Dante did any real thinking—that was not their job, and the relative value of the thought current at their time, the material forced upon each to use as the vehicle of his feeling, is of no importance.' Milton did what Shakespeare and Dante did: he made his poetry out of the thought current in his time. And Eliot believed that this was justified in the case of Shakespeare who, if he had written according to a better philosophy, 'would have written worse poetry: it was his business to express the greatest emotional intensity of his time, based on whatever his time happened to think'. Commenting on Dante's line:

la sua voluntade è nostra pace

Eliot wrote: 'It is great poetry and there is a great philosophy behind it.' Of Shakespeare's lines:

As flies to wanton boys, are we to the gods;
They kill us for their sport

he suggested that 'it is equally great poetry, though the philosophy behind it is not great'. Eliot found that Dante, with his acceptable philosophy, and Shakespeare, with his less great philosophy, both wrote great poetry, the essential thing being, as he saw it, 'that each expresses, in perfect language, some permanent human impulse'. In Eliot's view, the 'permanent human impulse' expressed by the poet is more relevant to a judgment of his poetry than the repugnance or attractiveness of his philosophy or theology. In spite of the fact that he saw Shakespeare's philosophy as 'the mixed and muddled scepticism of the Renaissance', he had no doubt that Shakespeare had transmuted it into great poetry. [17]

If Eliot's criterion is applied to Milton's work, the problem of the critic is not to decide whether Johnson was right in describing the narrative of *Paradise Lost* as truth, or whether Raleigh was right in calling the poem 'a monument to dead ideas'. The modern critic and the modern reader must, instead, explore the poetic results which Milton obtained from his material, and decide whether *Paradise Lost* expresses some such 'permanent human impulse' as that found by Eliot in the work of Shakespeare and Dante. F. T. Prince, in a comment on the supposed irrelevance to modern times of the ideas underlying Milton's epic, particularly the religious beliefs, suggested that 'we need not commit ourselves to any decision upon their truth or untruth, their lost or eternal validity. What matters to us as literary critics is what Milton has done with them, whether he has given them intellectual coherence, emotional depth, poetic force.' [18]

Frank Kermode's approach to Raleigh's description of the epic as a monument to dead ideas was to suggest that 'the poem is not a monument to any ideas'. A great deal of early praise for *Paradise Lost* had been inspired by the religious and edifying nature of the subject-matter: James Thorpe reports that in 1792 one writer maintained that the poem had contributed more to the support of the orthodox creed than all the books of divinity ever written. Much subsequent adverse criticism was based on dislike of the beliefs, or supposed beliefs, embodied in the epic. Kermode disapproved of both tendencies, suggesting that modern readers and critics need not follow either of these impulses. For him, as for Prince, the truth of the poem depended not upon the validity of the thought or on its modern relevance, but whether the myth had been turned into poetry: 'As much as any "barren philosophy precept"—to adapt Greville's expression—it must be turned into "pregnant images of life". Whether it is the Grail or Paradise, the truth of the poem depends upon

this process, not upon the special power of its theme.' Following
the kind of approach advocated by Eliot in *The Sacred Wood*, that
'when we are considering poetry we must consider it primarily
as poetry and not another thing', Kermode set out to correct
some of the defects which he believed were inherent in the work
of both defenders and critics of Milton's ideas. He argued that
'the modern reader has to agree not to indulge a special dis-
respect for Milton's myth; he should not despise it more than
any other that accounts for the origin of death'. On the other
hand, he believed that the modern reader must not be asked to
have a special respect for Milton's myth, for his theology, or for
his style, because he owes them 'no more than he owes the story
or the Hindu theology of *A Passage to India*, though of course he
owes them no less'.[19] If this is the correct approach, the really
important question for the critic to decide is whether Milton has
succeeded in transmuting his materials—whether these are naive
or especially sacred or both is irrelevant—into great epic poetry,
whether *Paradise Lost* is what Lascelles Abercrombie said an
epic poem ought to be, an exhibition of 'life in some great
symbolic attitude'.

So much for modern criticism of Milton's poem on the
grounds that twentieth-century readers are likely to find his
ideas repellent and uninteresting. As for the other complaint
which constantly recurs, that *Paradise Lost* is an inordinately
difficult poem requiring a range of learning and interests which
very few people now possess, it is difficult not to feel that it is
attended by a large element of exaggeration. Some outstanding
modern poems—which critics who find Milton's work obsolete
presumably consider much more readily accessible to modern
taste—require an even greater range of erudition and of reference than anything Milton ever wrote. Eliot's *Waste Land* may
be considered, to some extent at least, representative of modern
sensibility—from which Milton's work is supposed to be so
remote that, in John Wain's opinion, nothing short of 'a titanic
revolution of taste' will bring him back. *The Waste Land* has
quotations from, allusions to, or imitations of, at least thirty-
five different writers, ranging from Buddha and St Augustine to
F. H. Bradley and Baudelaire. Douglas Bush claimed that readers
of *The Waste Land* 'could not get very far before—and some did
not get very far after—they had read his notes and gained or
regained a pretty minute knowledge of Dante, Jessie Weston's
From Ritual to Romance, Frazer's *Golden Bough*, and a multitude of

casual items, like the Tarot pack of cards'. Bush contrasted Eliot's 'often arbitrary selection of more or less private symbols' with Milton's use of 'the central, mainly familiar and self-sufficient traditions of mankind'. [20]

The same critics who tell us that Milton's dependence on biblical materials and on the Christian tradition makes his poem inordinately difficult for the modern reader will cheerfully exhort us to master even more occult and esoteric sources in order to enjoy Eliot. And Yeats's poetry, we are frequently reminded, requires for its resolution a large body of ulterior knowledge: Buddhism, the Jewish Kabbala, the religion of Platonism, the Neoplatonic tradition of alchemy are all relevant. Milton's range of reference is admittedly wide: it is, however, the modern poets who require the footnotes and the commentaries.

Johnson once remarked that the perusal of *Paradise Lost* 'is a duty rather than a pleasure'. The spirit of this remark still pervades Milton criticism. Johnson's remark is not criticism: it is autobiography. It is an implied criticism of his own reading habits, and should perhaps be considered in conjunction with Boswell's statement that Johnson loved to read poetry, but hardly ever read any poem to an end. Modern critics who have mechanically echoed Johnson's duty–pleasure antithesis are perpetuating a false dilemma: the 'duty' of studying and mastering the difficulties of the poem is surely to be regarded as a prelude to the pleasure to be derived from an informed reading, and not as an alternative to pleasure. There can be few really great long poems which do not require some preliminary labour before they can be appreciated and enjoyed. And the aesthetic and historical claims of *Paradise Lost* are high enough to justify such labour.

CHAPTER SEVEN

'Paradise Lost': Milton's Intention and the Reader's Response

Almost since the appearance of *Paradise Lost* critics have had reservations about Milton's handling of his epic theme. Much early criticism was vague and incoherent: the twentieth century, however, has seen a systematic and thoroughgoing appraisal of the manner in which Milton treated his subject; the manner in which he accomplished, or failed to accomplish, his self-appointed task—*Paradise Lost* being generally regarded, and judged, as a poem with a purpose. Modern dissatisfaction with the narrative aspects of *Paradise Lost* is well documented: most of the main criticisms are lucidly set forth in Sir Walter Raleigh's *Milton* (1900), in A. J. A. Waldock's *'Paradise Lost' and its Critics* (1947), and in John Peter's *A Critique of 'Paradise Lost'* (1960). Of these attacks on Milton's presentation and treatment of the theme of the epic, that of Waldock has been the most influential. In his book he analyses the story and characterization of the poem in an attempt to show that Milton's theme presented him with problems which he had failed to solve, and that his failure has serious implications for his poem. Waldock found in *Paradise Lost* a damaging conflict between what the poem asserts, on the one hand, and what the poetry compels us to feel, on the other. He considered his findings so damaging that he dismissed the argument, the theme, the story of the epic as having little value, and claimed that the style alone stood between *Paradise Lost* and virtual oblivion. 'We shall', he suggested at the end of his critique, 'go on reading the poem for ever . . . for the glory of the writing and for the spirit of Milton that so lives in whatever he wrote.' But in the light of Waldock's own beliefs and assertions, this restriction of the value of the epic to its style and its embodiment of the spirit of Milton really amounted to small praise: earlier he had argued that 'when all is said the narrative problems are basic, for the poem is a story or it is nothing'.[1]

Waldock's critique has been given serious attention by most

critics of Milton's poetry who have written since 1947. Leavis endorsed his findings, and claimed that his book amounted to 'a radical criticism of *Paradise Lost*—a more damaging criticism than Professor Waldock himself recognizes'. Having elaborated his criticisms of the structure of the poem, Waldock had been prepared to allow that in its style *Paradise Lost* 'has enough left, in all conscience, to stay it against anything we can do'. But Leavis questioned even this concession: 'But what has it left?', he asked. 'There are the first two books, which are of a piece and grandly impressive, and, in the others, numbers of "beauties" major and minor.' He agreed that in *Paradise Lost* the balance is very badly disturbed, that there is a fatal conflict between feeling and theory, and he believed that Waldock's analysis had shown that 'Milton has so little self-knowledge and is so unqualified intellectually, that his intention (the intended significance of the poem) at the level of "justifying the ways of God to Men", and what he actually contrives as a poet to do, conflict, with disastrous consequences to both poem as such and intention.'[2] This is an excellent summary of Waldock's main argument. John Peter also endorsed Waldock's findings: in his own critique of the epic he described Waldock's book as 'second only to the text itself for a true understanding of the critical problems posed by the poem'.[3] Bernard Bergonzi, who could not endorse Waldock's findings, pointed to the serious implications of Leavis's combination of his own views on the style of the epic with those of Waldock on its structure, suggesting that if both language and structure are so unsatisfactory, then 'hardly anything worth considering of literary interest remains. . . . One might as well hand it over to philologists and historians of ideas'.[4]

Other critics considered Waldock's charges serious enough to merit detailed discussion, elaboration, or attempts at refutation. G. A. Wilkes devoted his work on *The Thesis of 'Paradise Lost'* almost entirely to answering Waldock's charges. They were discussed by Tillyard, Kermode and Professor Wright; the latter believed, with Waldock, that narrative problems were basic in *Paradise Lost*. He accepted Waldock's premises, but not his conclusions. Finally, Professor Empson's study of *Milton's God* (1961) threw some completely new light on the whole modern discussion of Milton's treatment of his epic material, and clarified many of the issues raised by Waldock.[5]

Waldock's criticisms of the poem are all made from the premise that it has an argument to expound, a thesis to make good, and that this argument is stated by Milton 'with unmistakable clarity and point'. There had been a good deal of controversy about the real theme of *Paradise Lost*: Waldock was in no doubt whatever that Addison had correctly described the real theme, the great moral, of the poem when he wrote:

'I am, however, of Opinion, that no just Heroic Poem ever was, or can be made from whence one great Moral may not be deduced. That which reigns in *Milton* is the most universal and most useful that can be imagined: it is in short this, that *Obedience to the Will of God makes Men happy, and that Disobedience makes them miserable*.'[6]

Waldock tested this argument, which he assumed to be the 'official' theme of the poem, in three principal ways. He tested it against Milton's treatment of God, against his presentation of the fall of Adam and Eve, and against his characterization of Satan. In all three cases he found a strong and damaging conflict between Milton's intentions and his performance, between 'the official significance of what happens and the natural bent of the narrative', as Frank Kermode put it. Milton clearly wishes to justify God's ways to men; what he actually achieves, according to Waldock, is something totally different: nothing short, in fact, of a justification of man's ways against God.

If Milton is to succeed in enforcing what Waldock assumes to be the moral of the whole poem, the reader must condemn Adam for his decision to share in the fall of Eve. But Milton's presentation of the Fall is such that we cannot condemn Adam. Thus, as Waldock sees it, at the very heart, the very centre, the crisis of a poem written to prove that God must at all times and in all circumstances be obeyed, the reader finds himself strongly sympathizing with an act of disobedience against God. In his treatment of the Fall, Milton overthrows his own argument, the argument on which he makes the success of his poem depend. This is the vital passage in which Adam announces his intention to share Eve's fall and to disobey God:

> How can I live without thee, how forgoe
> Thy sweet Converse and Love so dearly joind,
> To live again in these wilde Woods forlorn?
> Should God create another *Eve*, and I
> Another Rib afford, yet loss of thee
> Would never from my heart; no no, I feel

The link of Nature draw me: Flesh of Flesh,
Bone of my Bone thou art, and from thy State
Mine never shall be parted, bliss or woe.

IX. 908–916

It is on this passage that Waldock bases the kernel of his argument. In these lines, he argues, Adam is exemplifying 'one of the highest, and really one of the oldest, of all human values, selflessness in love'. Adam is faced with a conflict between this powerful human value and 'the mere doctrine that God must be obeyed'. Which is likely to have the greater influence on the feelings of the reader: Adam's exhibition of unselfish love, or an abstract doctrine? For Waldock, the answer is quite plain. On Milton's presentation of the case, all our sympathies are with Adam, who falls through love, 'not through sensuality, not through uxoriousness, not (above all) through gregariousness'. Milton has, in fact, made Adam's action in disobeying God seem worthy and honourable. 'Against the law', Waldock argues, 'against what is theoretically good, against God, he deliberately asserts what is for him a higher good and pursues it.'[7]

Thus, the current of the narrative in Book IX—which is the crisis of the poem for Waldock—is drawing the reader in a direction very different from that intended by Milton, who is, apparently, not always fully alive to the precise effect his narrative is having, not fully aware of what is happening to his argument. But Milton does realize sometimes, 'if vaguely', as Waldock puts it, that his material is getting out of hand. By this time, however, it is too late and the harm is done. His narration of the events of the Fall has made it difficult, if not impossible, for the reader to see Adam's action in an unfavourable light—and the success of Milton's thesis requires that he should. Then, Waldock argues, Milton, having realized that something has gone wrong, tries to set things right again by commenting on the events he has described in such a way as to induce the reader, whom the narrative has 'misled' into approving of Adam's course of action, to take the 'official' view of the events, to believe that in spite of the apparent nobility of Adam's action he must be condemned. This is Milton's comment on the fall of Adam, 'oddly out of harmony', according to Waldock, with his actual presentation of the event:

She gave him of that fair enticing Fruit
With liberal hand: he scrupl'd not to eat
Against his better knowledge, not deceav'd,
But fondly overcome with Femal charm.

IX. 996–999

Waldock is quite right to point out that 'fondly overcome with Femal charm' does not describe Adam's feelings as Milton earlier presented them. As his speech makes clear, his action is motivated by love. And the trouble is, as far as the success of Milton's thesis is concerned, that mere comments about 'Femal charm' cannot prevail with the reader against the nobility and selflessness which, in Milton's account of the episode, characterized Adam's decision to share Eve's fate. Here, as Waldock points out, we have 'a perfect example of the sort of clash that we must sometimes expect in *Paradise Lost* between Milton's theory of a matter and the matter as he has actually presented it'.[8] His theory, the 'official' view, can be discovered in his comments; these comments often conflict with the whole bent of the narrative which they are supposed to be interpreting. Thus the poem suffers from a continuous strain: Milton's demonstration of what is actually happening is pulling in one direction; his comments which often contradict the demonstration are pulling in another. And the poem, according to Waldock, cannot take the strain: it breaks under it at the critical juncture, because it 'asks from us, at one and the same time, two incompatible responses. It requires us . . . with the full weight of our minds to believe that Adam did right, and simultaneously requires us with the full weight of our minds to believe that he did wrong. The dilemma is as critical as that, and there is no way of escape.'[9]

The conflict between Milton's intention and the reader's response, between comment and demonstration, is felt most strongly in Book IX: the official view of the Fall is in utter conflict with the reader's sense of how and why it actually occurs. But, Waldock argues, this kind of conflict is not confined to Book IX: it is also to be found in Milton's treatment of Satan. Like the fall of Adam, the character of Satan gets beyond Milton's control. Waldock allows that in treating Satan Milton was faced with a very difficult problem. He must, for example, give him a reason for revolting, a reason that will not make him simply absurd. But, Waldock suggests, it must be a bad reason:

'the revolt must still be strange, unpardonable, abhorrent', because, we must remember, Milton's whole object is to justify obedience to the will of God. Again, to the detriment of his thesis, Milton allows the 'wrong' point of view to become far too attractive. Dealing with Satan's revolt, Waldock argues that Milton 'succeeded in suggesting a rather greater degree of provocation for it, and therefore of reasonableness in it, than he ever intended'. In the first two Books Satan exhibits 'fortitude in adversity, enormous endurance, a certain splendid recklessness, remarkable powers of rising to an occasion, extraordinary qualities of leadership . . . and striking in meeting difficulties that are novel and could seem overwhelming'.[10] Satan's attractiveness, in fact, soon threatens Milton's whole scheme, and Milton becomes nervous as he realizes this. To counteract the developing threat to his design he adopts the technique of comment which he later employs in dealing with the events of the Fall, the tenour of the comment being completely contrary to that of the presentation. After Satan's first speech—totally incompatible, as Waldock sees it, with despair—comes Milton's comment:

> So spake th' Apostate Angel, though in pain,
> Vaunting aloud, but rackt with deep despare.
>
> I. 125–126

There is, as Waldock observes, 'hardly a great speech of Satan's that Milton is not at pains to correct, to damp down and neutralize'. In the treatment of Satan, as in that of the Fall, we have the two levels: 'the level of demonstration or exhibition, and the level of allegation or commentary'. And between the two levels there is disagreement.[11]

Finally, there is Milton's presentation of God. If Satan is often made to appear too attractive for the good of Milton's thesis, God never is. The task of portraying God was bound to be one of extreme difficulty. A wiser poet than Milton would have been content to suggest rather than to present God. The best method, Waldock believes, would have been 'the tactful, prudent method of Dante with God—to keep him hidden: to lead us towards him, it may be, by degrees of mounting suspense, but to refuse the final revelation'. John Peter argues that God's presence is necessary in the poem but, he points out, 'it is reasonable to feel that everything possible should have been done to safeguard his presentation from miscarrying'.[12] Here, precisely, is where

Milton failed. Milton takes the grave risk of allowing us 'to stare God full in the face'; the real trouble is that he does not seem to have bothered to ensure that God should appear even moderately attractive. Quite the opposite, in fact, according to Waldock, who realizes that the very nature of the story must necessarily make God appear somewhat vindictive, but who suggests that Milton 'goes out of his way to convict him on his very first appearance of flagrant disingenuousness and hypocrisy'. And in Book III, Peter claims, 'God appears as a cruel tyrant whose equanimity can only be restored by the sacrifice of those who love him best'.[13]

Like most modern criticism of *Paradise Lost*, that of Waldock and Peter is not wholly original. It contains many elements which are to be found also in Shelley, Bagehot and Raleigh. Shelley, for example, in his *Defence of Poetry*, considered Milton's Satan as a moral being far superior to his God: he was able to avoid some of the conclusions later reached by Waldock by viewing the poem not as an attempt to justify obedience to God but as an implicit refutation of Christian belief. Bagehot is much closer to Waldock: like Waldock, he evaluated *Paradise Lost* as a poem with a thesis to make good, with a dogmatic aim, and like Waldock, he believed that Milton had failed to accomplish the task he had set himself. Bagehot anticipated Waldock's account of God and Satan. 'By a curiously fatal error', he remarked, 'Milton has selected for delineation exactly that part of the divine nature which is most beyond the reach of the human faculties. . . . He has made God argue. . . . His Satan was to him, as to us, the hero of his poem. . . . What a defect it is! especially what a defect in Milton's own view.'[14] Raleigh too regarded *Paradise Lost* as a poem written with a purpose in mind; he found Milton's God 'a whimsical Tyrant', the maker of 'arbitrary and occasional' laws; he described Satan as a 'splendid figure'; and he came to the conclusion that Milton had 'stultified the professed moral of his poem'.[15]

But in spite of such judgments, in spite of their belief that Milton had set himself a task in writing *Paradise Lost* which he had failed to accomplish, neither Raleigh nor Bagehot concluded that the faults they found were fatal to Milton's poem. Both were agreed that Milton had not succeeded in his attempt to justify obedience to the heart and imagination of the reader. They did not, however, press their arguments to their logical conclusion: they refrained from condemning the poem even though its performance did not live up to its professions. Waldock did not introduce much new evidence or formulate a wholly new approach; instead, working from the premises of previous critics, he developed their arguments more fully than they had done, and as a result, could not refrain from drawing the conclusions which Bagehot and Raleigh had failed to draw. And there is no gainsaying that if *Paradise Lost* is really a poem about the Fall of Man with a moral of obedience, Waldock's verdict that it is a failure is justified.

Has Waldock really made a serious case against *Paradise Lost*, and are his findings damaging enough to call in question the traditionally high estimate of the poem? Whatever we may think of Waldock's critique, his logic is flawless: if we accept his premises, we must accept his conclusions. Those who have tried to answer his criticisms of the poem have realized this: their attempts at refuting his argument have been directed towards undermining his premises, towards showing that his whole approach to the epic is fundamentally mistaken.

First of all, suppose we do accept his premises, and consequently his conclusions, what are the consequences of this for *Paradise Lost*? The first thing to bear in mind is that Waldock has a particular type of reader constantly before our eyes throughout his book. When he discusses the impressions we receive from *Paradise Lost*, he is really thinking of the impressions of his own ideal reader, defined by him as 'natural, easygoing, unprejudiced', who has 'acquired through the novel, and in other ways, certain types of literary experience that Milton was without'.[16] Waldock's ideal reader forms a very important part of his argument: it is through his eyes that we are expected to see *Paradise Lost*—his impressions, indeed, 'constitute the facts of the poem'. To understand Waldock's criticisms, then, we must try to understand the presuppositions and attitudes of his ideal reader, whose judgments of the poem Waldock expects us to share. The most important thing about Waldock's reader is his experience of narrative problems: he has derived from the novel—especially the post-Jamesian novel—a good deal of insight into such problems, insight which Milton lacked. He possesses a much more sophisticated technique than Milton did for assessing what Waldock calls 'the practicability of certain themes for literary treatment'. Judging *Paradise Lost*, as he is bound to judge it, in the light of his own experience as a novel-reader, he is liable to find it unsatisfactory from several points of view, and to find Milton singularly lacking in narrative instinct —since he so obviously failed to see that the material he chose to treat presented virtually insoluble problems. The modern reader will approach the poem expecting to find Milton 'thinking with his story'. Instead, he will find, as Waldock did, that Milton cannot think with his story for long, for whenever the natural bent of the narrative tends in the wrong direction— 'wrong' here meaning the official point of view already decided in advance—Milton hastens to rectify the deviation by means of a well-timed comment, designed to redirect the poem on to its proper course. Again, the modern reader is not likely to be satisfied with Milton's treatment of God, especially if what John Peter says is true. 'Milton's underlying assumption about the figure of God', he argues, 'is that it can be taken over intact from its context in the Bible or in Christian belief, and that there is little need to re-create it in the context of the poem'. [17] On the whole, Waldock's ideal modern reader is liable to find many of Milton's assumptions about narrative unfounded, and his disposition of his materials rather crude. Through no great merit of ours we have become far too expert in narrative techniques to be able to approve of Milton's performance, which we tend to find incompetent.

Thus, it seems, if we agree with Waldock to judge *Paradise Lost* as narrative from our standpoint as modern readers expert in fiction, we must find it sadly wanting. And if we agree with him that it is essentially a poem about the Fall written with the aim of justifying obedience, we must admit that it is largely a failure. There are serious criticisms, radical enough to call for a reconsideration of the status traditionally accorded to *Paradise Lost* by the great majority of critics. Before going on to consider some objections to Waldock's case against the poem, it might be well to examine some of his other assumptions. His ideal reader, it has already been pointed out, is expert in modern literary techniques, and will not hesitate to use his modern insights in evaluating *Paradise Lost*. He is also 'easygoing' and 'unprejudiced'. This, it transpires in the course of Waldock's discussion, means that he approaches the poem as if it were a modern naturalistic novel about real modern people. All that is necessary, according to Waldock, in reading the poem is to attend carefully to our impressions. He advocates—and presents—a reading which pays little or no attention to the background of the epic or to the conventions and beliefs underlying it. He feels, in fact, that attention to such factors can only interfere with 'our unforced sense of what is occurring'; that if we allow such things as the Christian tradition and seventeenth-century conventions to come between the poem and ourselves we are in danger of losing contact with the real *Paradise Lost* and of fabricating for ourselves a different poem. Waldock illustrates his approach most effectively in differing from C. S. Lewis in his account of the character of Adam. For Lewis, Milton's intentions must be considered when we are judging his performance: 'The first thing the reader needs to know about *Paradise Lost* is what Milton meant it to be.' Waldock put Lewis firmly in his place: 'Milton, Mr Lewis gathers, wished us to consider Adam as wise and great and kingly; very well, for Mr Lewis that settles the matter once and for all: Adam, whatever he may say or do, *is* wise and great and kingly.'[18] For Waldock, 'the facts of the poem' are identical with the impressions derived from it by readers whose responses are natural and spontaneous, uninhibited by promptings or instructions from critics who try to explain to them the kind of responses they ought to cultivate if they are to read the poem as Milton hoped they would. Waldock's whole approach is frankly unhistorical, even antihistorical. So far as his ideal reader is concerned, the researches of generations of commentators on the ideas underlying the poem might as well never have been undertaken, and scholarly elucidation of Milton's thought is at best an interesting irrelevance.

The most obvious answer to Waldock's kind of criticism— and the one most often encountered—is that his whole approach to the poem is mistaken, that his principles are wrong. He writes, his opponents point out, as if *Paradise Lost* were a kind of novel *manqué*, and not a seventeenth-century epic governed by conventions entirely different from those which govern the modern novel. He thus leaves genre and literary decorum completely out of account. More important still, perhaps, he reads *Paradise Lost*, as Bernard Bergonzi remarks, 'not merely as if Christianity were not true, but as though it had never existed'.[19] In his reading of the poem he refuses to avail of the insights and correctives which historical criticism provides: his ideal reader has no interest in the differences between seventeenth-century conventions of thought and feeling and those of our own time. As a result, the 'historical' critic will point out, he is bound to misread the poem. His monistic theory of narrative is probably the weakest point in his case: he asks us—and indeed the success of his argument requires us—to accept a conception of narrative designed to embrace both the modern novel and the seventeenth-century epic. But surely, one might well argue, the one conception of narrative cannot possibly be made to fit both genres. This is Bernard Bergonzi's main objection to Waldock's case. The modern novel, he points out, 'deals, for the most part with men, and in their fallen state, rather than supernatural or pre-lapsarian beings. Behaviour in the novel is inevitably involved with a complex of assumptions relating to the existing order of society, and the conventions governing the form are all intensely naturalistic.' Since any concept of narrative derived from the novel must be affected by such conditions, it would, Bergonzi suggests, 'be wholly inapplicable to such a poem as *Paradise Lost*'.[20]

The historical approach leads to a wholly different interpretation of almost every aspect of the poem from that offered by Waldock. In his account of Milton's presentation of the fall of Adam, for example, he argues that Adam, in electing to share Eve's fate, 'seems to us—he seems to Milton, although Milton is not in a position to admit it—to be doing a worthy thing'. Rajan, however, in a study of the poem which appeared about the same time as Waldock's, and in which the author takes the Christian tradition and the seventeenth-century intellectual background fully into account, presents an entirely different interpretation of Adam's action: 'We cannot approve of what Adam does and we can approve still less the alacrity with which he does it. There is in him no will, no power of resisting temptation. . . . His idolatry, all the more offensive because it is clear-eyed, is an insult to the righteousness to which he is meant to conform.'[21] This, at any rate, is how Milton's seventeenth-century reader would interpret the fall of Adam: if we see it as Waldock does, this means that our sensibilities are different from those of the seventeenth-century reader whom Milton presumably had in mind when he was writing *Paradise Lost*. It also means, according to the 'historical' critics, that our response to this vital part of Milton's poem is a mistaken one, which must be corrected. To ensure that our responses to the Fall are 'correct', C. S. Lewis points out that Milton's version is substantially that of St Augustine, which is that of the Church as a whole. 'By studying this version', he argues, 'we shall learn what the story meant in general to Milton and to his contemporaries and shall thus be the more likely to avoid various false emphases to which modern readers are liable.' He then goes on to explain St Augustine's version of the Fall.[22] If we are prepared to accept the argument that the historical approach to *Paradise Lost* is the only valid one, the problems concerning Milton's intention and the reader's response disappear almost completely. For critics like C. S. Lewis and Douglas Bush, Satan never becomes attractive enough to threaten Milton's design. Unlike Waldock, they do not feel that the reader is bound to approve of Adam's decision to share in Eve's fall. For them, the reader's response is in harmony with Milton's intention: it could hardly be otherwise, since they plead for a reading of the poem which takes full account of that intention.

In a sense, historical criticism provides an answer to Waldock's kind of argument; for many critics it provides a convincing and decisive answer. The difficulty remains, however, that for others historical criticism has no finality: numerous influential critics believe that a poem should be approached with the least possible attention to its intellectual and historical background; they, at any rate, would hardly be convinced by a predominantly 'historical' defence of the poem against Waldock's—and indeed Raleigh's and Bagehot's—strictures. Most of the attempts to answer Waldock have not really disposed of his arguments: they have merely transferred the discussion from the level of literary criticism to that of critical theory, where we must try to adjudicate or decide between conflicting approaches, evaluative assumptions, or even philosophies.

The critic who has shown the most actue awareness of this difficulty has been G. A. Wilkes. In his answer to Waldock, he points out that the arguments about Milton's intention and the reader's response can never really be settled at the level of general critical theory. He argues, however, that 'the central issue, whether or not Milton's epic performs what it promises', can be decided substantially by an appeal to 'what happens' in the poem. An answer along such lines, in fact, is the only one which could really satisfy Waldock, whose whole argument was conducted at the level of 'what happens' in *Paradise Lost*. Wilkes is prepared to make some interesting and important concessions to Waldock. He freely recognizes the hindrances to Milton's design, 'the unsympathetic presentation of God, the seductive appeal of Satan, the nobility of Adam in his wrongful choice'. He is even prepared to admit, for the sake of argument, that Waldock's reading of the Fall episode is correct, and that our sympathy goes to Adam in his act of disobedience against God.[23]

But even if Waldock's most serious charge is admitted—the charge that the reader instinctively approves of Adam's act of disobedience—does this really mean, as Waldock claims it does, that the poem breaks at its centre. It does, according to Wilkes, only if the Fall *is* the centre of *Paradise Lost*, 'the climactic point at which the thesis meets its severest trial'. Waldock's argument depends on this assumption. But critics like Waldock, who write as if the whole meaning of the poem were concentrated in single features like the figure of Satan or the Fall, are, as Wilkes points out, losing sight of the total scheme of *Paradise Lost*. To write about the epic as if it were simply a poem about obedience with its 'crisis' in Book IX is to act without any warrant from the text. Those who judge *Paradise Lost* as a poem written to justify obedience are really dealing with a poem of their own which they have abstracted from the real *Paradise Lost*: in asking us to consider the epic as a treatment of the disobedience and fall of man they are, in effect, asking us to ignore completely Books V to VIII. Wilkes argues that 'the only formula that is adequate to Milton's declared intention, and that comprehends the whole text, is that *Paradise Lost* is a treatment of the operation of Providence, traced through the celestial cycle from the revolt of the angels to the Last Judgement, and its purpose is to justify the workings of Providence to mankind'.[24]

It is far more, then, than a poem about obedience, it deals with man's recovery of Paradise as well as with his loss of it; and, as a careful reading of the whole text makes clear, even the Fall and the Redemption are only elements in an even larger pattern, a more massive structure. How then must our sympathy with Adam be measured? Against the scheme of the twelve books, according to Wilkes. And seen against the background of the total scheme of the poem—the celestial cycle—the reader's sympathy for Adam and Satan become merely local difficulties, not fatal flaws in the design of the poem. And *Paradise Lost* cannot break at the centre, because it has no centre. 'The weight of Milton's conception', as Wilkes shows, 'is not poised on one episode analysed by Professor Waldock, or on another singled out by Dr Tillyard: its weight is distributed through the whole structure, and all twelve books of the poem help to support it.' And, he points out, 'whether or not we concede Waldock's reading of the Fall does not greatly matter, for the dilemma he presents is finally irrelevant. His whole argument rests on an assumption about Milton's purpose that is not borne out by the text, and his dilemma has its existence in a poem fabricated from *Paradise Lost*.'[25]

Wilkes has undoubtedly provided a convincing refutation of Waldock's main argument, and he has done so without any appeal to general critical theory: his defence of *Paradise Lost* is firmly grounded on the text. But it is often not enough, especially when Milton's epic characters are under discussion, merely to pay close attention to the text unless it is constantly borne in mind that *Paradise Lost* is a poem: far too many critics have discussed it as if it were a logical demonstration in prose form. John Peter makes an interesting point about criticisms of Adam and Eve; he points out that these criticisms 'often turn out to be unreal, conceivably justified by subsequent and abstract reflection, but not by the impact of the poetry as we read it.'[26] The same critic suggests that one of the commonest faults in Milton criticism 'is to wrench the characters and incidents of *Paradise Lost* from their artistic context . . . disregarding the significance which has been conferred upon them by the poem'.[27] This is an extremely important observation—and, on the whole, a just one. The tendency to isolate the characters of the epic from their poetical settings, to refuse to submit them to the current of the narrative, is not peculiar to any one group of critics; it is to be found in Shelley, Bagehot, Raleigh and Waldock as well as in Bush, Lewis and Professor Wright. This tendency is perhaps best studied in the various critical treatments of the character of Satan.

Satan, if he is isolated from his background in the epic and viewed as an independent entity—and if his faults are ignored—may arouse intense admiration. If he is seen, on the other hand, as Milton actually presents him, against the background of the whole poem, then his heroic qualities, presented in their evil context, appear far less admirable than they do if Satan is allowed to exist outside the context of the poem. Much of the criticism of Milton's Satan is strongly reminiscent of the Shakespearean criticism of Bradley, who tended to examine the characters of Shakespeare's plays as if their existence were independent of the works in which they appeared. It is not really important, as far as Milton's success in *Paradise Lost* is concerned, whether a Bradley-type prose account of Satan is more attractive than a similar account of God. It is important, however, to discover whether Milton has succeeded in embodying Satan's evil nature poetically throughout the poem as a whole: whether *Paradise Lost* enacts for its readers its moral valuations.

This is the kind of problem that has been neglected by many critics of *Paradise Lost*. Professor Wright represents one rather strong tendency when he argues, in trying to defend the integrity of the poem, that 'we shall not be likely to misread the story if this fact is kept in mind—that Satan and his fellows are evil'. There are strong reasons for not accepting Wright's argument; his suggestion is like Sir Herbert Tree's remark about the character of Macbeth. 'We must interpret Macbeth', he wrote, 'before and at the crisis, by his just and equitable character as a king that history gives him.'[28] But the work of the adverse critics has scarcely provided the perfect corrective to this kind of approach. It is true that Bagehot, Raleigh and Waldock do not try to substitute the Satan of Christian tradition for Milton's Satan. The figure described by Raleigh is, in a sense, the real Satan of *Paradise Lost*. 'Milton', he believes, 'is far indeed from permitting us to think him a fool. The nobility and greatness of his bearing are brought home to us in some half-dozen of the finest poetic passages in the world.'[29] And yet there is equally good evidence in the poem for C. S. Lewis's remarks about Satan's 'design of ruining two creatures who had never done him any harm'.[30] Satan as seen by Lewis is far indeed from the 'august creature' described by Landor, or the 'splendid figure' seen by Raleigh.

Character sketches of God, Satan, Adam and Eve—based on information derived from the poem—could be augmented almost indefinitely. But, it might be asked, could they really tell us anything about the problem which they are being used to solve, whether Milton's portrayal of Satan throws the poem radically off balance and stultifies its professed moral? L. C. Knights made some remarks on Shakespeare's plays which are also relevant to Milton's epic. The 'total response' he speaks of has received little attention from critics of *Paradise Lost*. 'The total response to a Shakespeare play', he suggests, 'can only be obtained by an exact and sensitive study of the quality of the verse, of the rhythm and imagery, of the controlled associations of the words and their emotional and intellectual force, in short by an exact and sensitive study of Shakespeare's handling of language.'[31]

Critics who have tried to show, by contrasting 'abstracted'

characters, that Milton's poem is unbalanced, have largely ignored the factors mentioned by Knights. One factor of great importance in this connection is the evaluative function of Milton's imagery. When critics like Bagehot and Raleigh listed in cold prose the qualities of Satan—qualities which, they supposed, endangered Milton's design—they were ignoring the precautions which he had taken to preserve the integrity of his poem. The prose character-sketches did not take account of the way in which Milton handles Satan in the poem, the subtle manner in which he uses imagery to move the reader to horror, scorn, amazement, repulsion. And since *Paradise Lost* is first and foremost a poem, Milton's success or failure in making his thesis appeal to the imagination of the reader ought to be judged in poetic terms, and not on the evidence of a prose analysis. An examination of the evaluative imagery of the poem shows how Milton directs the responses of his readers—those at least who are willing to respond to the poetry—to the protagonists. If we ignore the use to which Milton puts his Epic Similes, what Professor Wright calls 'the ridicule that underlies even his most enchanting pictures of the fallen angels', we are ignoring an important piece of evidence. The function of the poetry in forwarding Milton's design has been virtually ignored by adverse critics of the poem.

Of all the hindrances to Milton's design, his presentation of God is the greatest; even the stoutest defenders of the poem have expressed dissatisfaction with the God of *Paradise Lost*. The faults in Milton's presentation are obvious enough, and have provided hostile critics with plenty of ammunition. He has made God argue; according to Waldock he has convicted Him of 'flagrant disingenuousness and hypocrisy'; and in Book III, John Peter claims, 'God appears as a cruel tyrant whose equanimity can only be restored by the sacrifice of those who love him best'.[32] Such criticisms could be multiplied.

In the end, however, Milton's presentation of God, however unsatisfactory we may judge it to be, must be seen in perspective: it must be assessed in relation to the poem as a whole, and not discussed as if the success or failure of *Paradise Lost* depended on a 'sympathetic' or 'likeable' God. Wilkes points out that Milton's God fulfils more than one role: he is an agent in the poem as well as a character, and as an agent 'he is the author and disposer of the vast operation that absorbs evil and converts it into greater good'.[33]

Since 1900, when Sir Walter Raleigh's book on Milton appeared, successive critics have brought some really fundamental criticism to bear on the narrative problems of *Paradise Lost*. Whether their criticism has been hostile or favourable, all of them have contributed to our understanding of the poem. To discuss adverse criticism of the structure of *Paradise Lost* primarily in terms of Waldock's critique is not, one hopes, to give him an undue eminence among Miltonists, or even to set him up as an arch anti-Miltonist. His examination of the epic as a narrative poem is important because he has developed the hostile criticisms of Bagehot and Raleigh to their fullest extent, pointed out the consequences of their findings, and drawn the conclusions they failed to draw. In a real sense, he has brought discussion of *Paradise Lost* up to date by trying to show how the poem fares when considered against the background of twentieth-century literary techniques.

CHAPTER EIGHT

Tyrannic Power

Milton's influence on English poetry has, since the early eighteenth century, often been described as baneful, but until the early twentieth century this influence was never regarded as a really serious ground for condemnation. There was never any suggestion of a reassessment of his position on the ground that his work was no longer a fruitful source of inspiration for practising poets. It may of course be true that the reason for this was that for more than two centuries most poets found fruitful inspiration in Milton's work. It is certainly true that the tendency to assess the poets of the past on their relevance to those of the present did not enter English criticism for the first time with Eliot and Pound. We find it in Wordsworth, who regarded Pope in much the same way as Eliot regarded Milton. It is also to be found in Coleridge, another poet-critic, who was acutely conscious of using the work of older poets to help solve the problems of the poets of the Romantic Revival. George Watson has pointed out that 'Coleridge does not recommend the older English poets for their own virtues: his concern . . . is to unite their "characteristic merits" with those of his own age in an ideal poetic language'.[1] This unification helped to bring about a revolution in poetry. To the poet-critics who launched the twentieth-century revolt against a devitalized tradition, 'influence' was again an important factor in judging the poets of the past, and poets like Eliot made a clear distinction between 'good' poets whose influence was considered beneficial, and 'great' poets who, although they might have triumphed over language, could not be fruitfully imitated or echoed by the modern poet. In his first essay on Milton (who, in the sense just mentioned, was 'great' rather than 'good') Eliot claimed that 'it is more important, in some vital respects, to be a good poet than to be a great poet'.[2]

Although both Coleridge and Eliot both looked at Milton from the same standpoint—their concern with his poetry was 'pragmatic' rather than 'objective'—their conclusions about the value of his work were totally different. For Coleridge, Milton was worthy of admiration not only on the strength of his poetry, but also because of his power of radiation. He never doubted that Milton could be a valuable stimulus to the poets of the early nineteenth century: in his own poetry he put his belief in Milton's good influence into practice. His poem *Dejection: An Ode* is a good example; the first line comes from *Samson Agonistes*, and the rhythm of the stanza is that of the *Nativity Ode*:

> My genial spirits fail;
> And what can these avail
> To lift the smothering weight from off my breast?
> It were a vain endeavour,
> Though I should gaze for ever
> On that green light that lingers in the west:
> I may not hope from outward forms to win
> The passion and the life, whose fountains are within.

Eliot's view of Milton's influence was, in his early criticism at least, entirely unfavourable. Unlike Coleridge, he could not recommend Milton as an example for imitation by his fellow-poets. On the contrary, he claimed that Milton 'may still be considered as having done damage to the English language from which it has not wholly recovered'.[3]

Concern about the dangers involved in the imitation of Milton can be traced back to the beginnings of Milton criticism. In 1723 Pope found fault with the 'dramatic' parts of *Paradise Lost* where, he claimed, 'there is frequently such transposition and forced construction that the very sense is not to be discovered without a second or third reading', and, he added, 'in this certainly he ought to be no example'. John Dennis felt it necessary to refer in detail to certain defects in Milton's style, because, as he put it, 'some of them ought to be avoided with the utmost Caution, as being so great, that they would be Insupportable in any one who had not his extraordinary Distinguishing Qualities'. Hazlitt echoed Dennis; only a writer of Milton's genius could hope to imitate his work with real success. Any other blank verse but Milton's, according to Hazlitt (and he includes Thomson's, Young's, Cowper's and Wordsworth's), 'will be found, for the want of the same insight into "the hidden soul of harmony", to be mere lumbering prose'. And Raleigh claimed that Milton left a highroad behind him along which many a tuneful pauper has since limped.[4]

But critics who drew attention to the dangers of Milton's

influence were usually careful to lay the blame on the poets who were influenced rather than on Milton's style. Pope censured Milton's imitators for failing to derive real benefit from their study of his work. He found fault with them, above all, for failing to realize that Milton is 'not lavish of his exotic words and phrases every where alike'. The Miltonic verse which so many of them produced was not so much a copy as a caricature of their original, being 'a hundred times more obsolete and cramp' than Milton's. Most of the eighteenth- and nineteenth-century critics would have agreed with the judgment of Havens, who censured Thomson for not using Milton with discretion and propriety: 'A great deal of Thomson's tumidity came from his adopting, without sufficiently adapting, Milton's practice.'[5] Imitators like Thomson adopted Milton's manner without realizing that the kind of style which befitted angelic debates and heavenly wars was not necessarily appropriate to descriptions of Musidora's bathing or the shearing of sheep.

In his first essay on Milton, Eliot put forward a fundamentally different theory of Milton's influence and its significance than that previously accepted. He repeated, in a more extreme form, the views of previous critics, finding more of Milton's influence in the badness of the bad verse of the eighteenth century than of anybody else's, transferring much of the obloquy which had fallen on Dryden and Pope to Milton. Some years earlier Eliot had adduced Milton's influence as one of the primary causes of the notorious 'dissociation of sensibility'. Like most previous critics, Eliot realized that the charge of bad influence was not necessarily a serious one; it could, after all, be dismissed by saying that the poets of the eighteenth century were so bad that they could be influenced only for the worse. But Eliot was not prepared to leave the matter there: he departed fundamentally from the traditional view of Milton's influence when he suggested that there was a more serious charge to be made against Milton than critics from Pope to Raleigh had been prepared to make: 'Milton's poetry', Eliot suggested, 'could only be an influence for the worse upon any poet whatever.'[6]

This suggestion that bad influence was a permanent characteristic of Milton's poetry amounted, in the opinion of those critics who judged poets of the past in terms of their usefulness to those of the present, to a serious charge against Milton. The totally adverse view of Milton's influence expressed by Eliot seemed all the more damaging to Milton's reputation in the critical milieu which Eliot himself helped to fashion. Leavis, writing of Donne, found that his work had the very quality, denied to Milton by Eliot, which was so important to so many twentieth-century critics. Leavis wrote of 'the extraordinary force of originality that made Donne so potent an influence in the seventeenth century' and suggested that the same originality 'makes him now at once for us, without his being the less felt as of his period, contemporary—obviously a living poet in the most important sense'.[7] Milton, viewed in the light of Eliot's judgment on his influence—'against which we still have to struggle'—was at the farthest possible remove from the living poet admired by Leavis. And the full implication of the reference to 'a living poet in the most important sense' was made clear by Leavis when he wrote of the poetry of the past that 'its life is in the present or nowhere; it is alive in so far as it is alive for us'.[8]

The most detailed exposition of the case against Milton on the ground of his bad influence was by Middleton Murry, whose approach was similar to Eliot's. His interest in the problems of the creative writer of the present day led him to consider which poets of the past could best offer example and stimulation to those of the present. Shakespeare, he concluded, could be of help to the aspiring modern poet; Milton was a poet to avoid. Murry's attitude was strongly influenced by his sympathetic interest in Keats who, to unfortunate effect as Murry saw it, had so 'penetrated into the process of the Miltonic style'. Keats has been cast, by Murry and others, in the role of tragic victim of Miltonic prepotence. Milton's influence, on the first *Hyperion* above all, led Keats in the wrong direction: there was death for him in Milton, his true and natural line of development was arrested. Penetration into Milton could produce only Miltonics but, Murry suggested, penetration into Shakespeare was bound to have a far different result: not, surprisingly enough, the production of imitation Shakespeare but a knowledge of, and a feeling for, 'the vital processes of style'.[9] This kind of argument patently contradicts the facts: Keats did penetrate into Shakespeare, but to no greater advantage to his poetry than that derived from his study of Milton. If *Hyperion* was produced under the shadow of Milton, *Otho the Great* was written in the Shakespearean manner. *Hyperion* has considerable merit; *Otho the Great* has very little.

Eliot's and Murry's remarks were echoed by many other critics; Leavis pointed out that the twentieth-century revolution in poetry was to a great extent a movement away from Milton's influence which had, as he saw it, predominated to unfortunate effect in various forms from Thomson 'through Gray, Cowper and Akenside to Wordsworth and though allied with Spenser, through Keats and Tennyson'. As a desirable alternative Leavis supported 'the reopening of communications with the seventeenth century of Shakespeare, Donne, Middleton, Tourneur and so on'.[10] Bonamy Dobrée contrasted Milton's bad influence with Dryden's beneficial effect on English poetry, suggesting that whereas Dryden made the language 'miraculously flexible', Milton made it 'stiff and tortuous, even distorted, unusable in that form by other poets as Keats was to discover'.[11]

Such censures of Milton's influence posed problems for those who wrote in his defence. It is significant that very few of the critics who tried to answer the charge of bad influence were themselves poets. This explains, to some extent at least, why critics like Tillyard, Grierson and Bush, not being quite as conscious as Eliot and Pound were of the importance of the past as a stimulus to the present, tended to dismiss the arguments of the adverse critics as being of little importance except to practising poets. It is true that two of Milton's staunchest modern defenders, Charles Williams and C. S. Lewis, were poets, but although they wrote in the twentieth century they are not contemporary in the same way that Eliot is: Leavis rightly places the work of Williams in the same tradition as *The Testament of Beauty*. And Lewis was so radically out of sympathy with his time that he closed his eyes completely to modern developments in poetry.

There has been a tendency among Milton's academic defenders to doubt whether the influence of any poet on his successors, whether that influence has been baneful or beneficial, can properly be adduced as a factor in an assessment of his greatness. Modern attacks on Milton's bad influence have therefore not seemed as important or as damaging as have the adverse criticisms of his epic style. As a result, although much has been written in modern times in defence of Milton's style, comparatively little has been written in defence of the influence of that style. Grierson's reaction to modern disapproval of Milton's influence was typical: he felt that although Eliot and others may have had perfectly sound reasons for deploring Milton's influence, this could tell us absolutely nothing about Milton's poetry itself. 'A work of art', Grierson claimed, 'is not thus relative. It is absolute, self contained.'[12] Grierson was evidently not familiar with Eliot's doctrine of Tradition. Other critics shared Grierson's views; Tillyard argued that it does not follow that Marlowe is worthless because Gray and his contemporaries owed nothing to his influence, and Bush pointed out that 'we should hesitate to blame Mr Eliot for the not always successful efforts of his imitators'.[13]

There is no real answer to the arguments just quoted. But at the same time it must be pointed out that they do not meet the case, which was presented on a different level. The clash of views arises out of a double standard: attackers and defenders are not really arguing about the same thing. Tillyard's use of 'worthless' illustrates this. He uses the word in an absolute sense: none of Milton's adverse critics suggested, even remotely, that Milton was worthless in this sense. The suggestion was that Milton was worthless to modern poets in their quest for a new kind of poetry. This, at any rate, was Eliot's suggestion, and in making it he appealed, appropriately enough, not to critics but to practising poets: 'And of what I have to say I consider that the only jury of judgment is that of the ablest poetical practitioners of my own time.'[14]

In its most extreme form, the modern case against Milton on the ground of bad influence amounted to the suggestion that Milton could never, under any circumstances, be anything but a bad influence on English poetry. From the point of view expressed by Grierson—the point of view that a work of art is 'absolute, self-contained'—this did not amount to a serious charge. But from another point of view it did. If accepted, it imposed certain limitations on Milton; for one thing, it seemed to deprive his work of all possibility of a living currency, even for the future. If Milton could never again stimulate poets, he might never again stimulate the kind of 'living criticism' which poets of different ages write about their fellow poets of ages past, and which is possibly the greatest factor in keeping the poets of the past 'alive' for the present. If being alive for the present has anything to do with our judgment of a poet, then it must be admitted that the comments of practising poets merit a good deal more attention than they have received from some of Milton's apologists.

But the case against Milton's bad influence has become somewhat less important, and its validity has been impaired, since Eliot, the critic who first gave it a wide currency, took it upon himself to undermine it. In his second essay on Milton, which appeared in 1947, he answered the more extreme hostile comments on Milton's influence—including his own. In this second essay he made two really important points: the first signified a return on his part to the traditional view of Milton's influence, which he had earlier hoped to undermine, the view that 'the responsibility, if there be any, is rather with the poets who were influenced than with the poet whose work exerted the influence'.[15] Even more important was his suggestion that modern poets need no longer avoid Milton's influence, that they could, in fact, derive much benefit from the study of his work. He argued that the poetry of the rest of this century 'might have much to learn from Milton's extended verse structure' and that a study of *Samson Agonistes* 'should sharpen anyone's appreciation of the justified irregularity, and put him on guard against the pointless irregularity'.[16]

In these remarks Eliot was entirely straightforward and unambiguous: there was no suggestion of irony. It is quite plain that they amount to a radical change of mind about Milton on Eliot's part since he wrote his first essay in 1935. The second essay is much more than a qualified retraction. Yet very few people are prepared to accept Eliot's later remarks at their face value, plain and unambiguous as they are. Leavis, for example, refused to believe that Eliot's second essay represented a serious change of opinion, suggesting that those who read it in this light can 'never have taken an intelligent interest in his poetry'.[17]

Eliot's revised views on Milton disturbed those critics, among them Leavis, who had so loyally and steadfastly followed his earlier line. And there is one modern poet, admired, indeed revered, by many of the critics to whom Milton's bad influence is an article of faith, who poses a rather awkward problem for those among his admirers who have assisted in Milton's dislodgment. It may be stretching things a little to describe Hopkins as a modern poet—he died in 1889—but he has, at any rate, been enlisted by Leavis in the ranks of the living poets, alongside Eliot and Pound. Hopkins greatly admired Milton's poetry; he praised Milton for, of all things, his use of 'the current language' of his age, 'heightened . . . but not an obsolete one'. Here Hopkins is challenging, in fact flatly contradicting, a fundamental belief of his modern admirers: that Milton's language is never current and always obsolete.

But Hopkins did more than merely admire Milton's language

and versification—he claimed several times that Milton was his model: 'I have paid a good deal of attention to Milton's versification and collected his later rhythms. . . . Milton is the great standard in the use of counterpoint. . . . I hope in time to have a more balanced and Miltonic style'.[18] Hopkins, in one of his letters to Dixon, related his study of Milton's last poems to his own technical experiments. He considered the choruses of *Samson Agonistes* the 'highwater mark' of Milton's versification, 'Milton having been not only ahead of his own time as well as all after-times in verse-structure'. It is clear that his study of *Samson Agonistes* had a bearing on the evolution of his own rhythms: the choruses, he suggested, 'are . . . counterpointed throughout; that is, each line (or nearly so) has two different coexisting scansions. But when you reach that point the secondary or "mounted rhythm", which is necessarily a sprung rhythm, overpowers the original or conventional one and then this becomes superfluous and may be got rid of; by taking this last step you reach simple sprung rhythm.'[19] Critics may find it difficult to detect Miltonic influence in Hopkins's language; they ought to be prepared, however, to take his word for it that the study of Milton influenced his versification.

Some critics from whom one would expect comment have fought shy of this topic. One critic, Donald Davie, has, however, dealt with it rather fully, and his attitude to Hopkins's remarks on Milton is reminiscent of Leavis's determination not to believe, in spite of an overwhelming weight of evidence, that Eliot had changed his mind about Milton as an influence on modern poetry. Davie feels that Hopkins's praise of Milton's poetry must be explained: after all, as he points out, Hopkins 'challenges one of the best authenticated working principles in the English poetic tradition—the principle that Milton, however great in himself, is a bad example for other poets'.[20] After some discussion he explains, or rather explains away, Hopkins's admiration. Hopkins, it seems—his own clear testimony to the contrary notwithstanding—did not really admire Milton's style at all. 'One is forced to the conclusion', Davie argues, 'that it was just this, Milton's egotism, individualism and arrogance, which made him for Hopkins the model poet'.[21] One is not forced to any such conclusion: 'Don't like what you say of Milton, I think he was a very bad man: those who, contrary to our Lord's command, both break themselves and, as St Paul says, consent to those who break themselves the sacred bond of marriage, like

Luther and Milton, fall with open eyes into the terrible judgment of God' (Hopkins to Robert Bridges). Hopkins admired Milton the poet, not Milton the man.

Dispirited Miltonists, tired of reading about the harm done to English poetry by Milton's influence and example, can derive some comfort and satisfaction from T. J. B. Spencer's interesting lecture, 'The Tyranny of Shakespeare'. Spencer points out that in the course of the nineteenth century more and more poets attempted to use Shakespeare's language, 'and suffered the consequences of their temerity'. Byron regarded Shakespeare as 'the *worst* of models'. Arnold's attitude is adequately summed up by Spencer in what amounts to a clever parody of Eliot's early remarks on Milton:

'In brief, Arnold had serious charges to make against Shakespeare, in respect of the deterioration—the peculiar kind of deterioration—to which he subjected the language. He could be considered as having done damage to the English poetic language from which it had not wholly recovered.'[22]

So far, almost all the stress has been on Milton's 'bad' influence. This is only natural: we have been conditioned by our modern myth-makers to see Milton as the personification of all that modern poetry had to renounce in order to recover its health. But undue emphasis on the problems of twentieth-century poets and on the crisis in modern poetry has led to a serious loss of balance and perspective. Milton's influence is far more profitably considered against a larger background: the history of the development of English poetry since the late seventeenth century. It is unfortunate that Milton's leading adverse critics have gloried in their status as 'literary critics' and have exhibited varying degrees of contempt for scholars and historians of literature. It is from the despised scholars and historians, however, that we get the balance and sense of perspective so sadly lacking in the work of some of the merely 'literary' critics: especially on such a subject as Milton's influence.

There is one aspect of Milton's influence on English poetry which has not received sufficient attention in modern times: his almost solitary defence and maintenance of the dignity of poetry against the almost overwhelmingly hostile pressures of the age in which he wrote. Professor Willey's analysis of the problems of the Heroic poet in the age of the Royal Society prompts one to shift the emphasis from Milton's bad influence to the in-

debtedness of English poetry to Milton. His appearance at a
vital stage in the seventeenth century was fortunate for poetry:
he 'reasserted its greatness and its divine origin', as Ifor Evans
pointed out, at a time when scientific and philosophical developments were threatening its prestige. Willey adduces a great deal
of evidence to show that 'truth' was being handed over more and
more to philosophy 'with prose as its proper medium, while
poetry was being reduced to the role of catering for delight by
means of agreeable images . . .'[23] Milton's last poems are a trium-
phant answer to those of his contemporaries like Hobbes who
denigrated poetry. In *Leviathan* Hobbes included 'the use of
Metaphors, Tropes, and other Rhetoricall figures, in stead of
words proper' among the causes of 'Absurd conclusions'. It is
hardly too much to say that Milton, single-handed, gave poetry
a new lease of life. His influence, instead of being a subject of
censure, might well become one of the chief grounds for
admiration if considered in relation to the precarious position of
poetry when his last poems were being published.

CHAPTER NINE

Summing Up

Milton's modern critics have concentrated their attention on *Paradise Lost*. There has been no major questioning of the traditional appraisal of the minor poems; the tendency, on the contrary, has been to express regret that Milton did not continue, after *Lycidas*, to write as he had written in *Comus*, a work praised by Dr Leavis for its comparative sensuous richness. The only poem, apart from *Paradise Lost*, that came in for any significant adverse comment was *Samson Agonistes*, in which, Middleton Murry believed, Milton's poetic vitality was at its lowest, and of which Leavis asked: 'How many cultivated adults could honestly swear that they had read it through with enjoyment?'[1]

The most important question arising from the Milton Controversy is whether the case made by the hostile critics provides grounds for a rejection, or at least a substantial modification, of the nineteenth-century view of Milton as a twin peak with Shakespeare. Ezra Pound's answer was forthright, if somewhat intemperate; he suggested that Milton's real place was nearer to Drummond of Hawthornden than to Shakespeare. T. S. Eliot, on the other hand, described Shakespeare and Milton as 'our two greatest poets'. Most of the other critics who have, at various times, come out against Milton, have been singularly unwilling to consider the effect of modern criticism on his position among the English poets. Dr Leavis has written of Milton's 'dislodgment' and has constantly implied that he was overvalued in the past; he has, however, refused to commit himself to any new 'placing'—something he felt able to do in the case of Dryden, whom he contrasted unfavourably with 'the incomparably greater Pope'. John Peter was extremely evasive: he cited Peacock's view that Milton was a greater poet than Shakespeare, but went on to suggest, rather unhelpfully, that 'to disagree with Peacock it is hardly necessary to set Milton lower than Cowley or Gray or Rupert Brooke'.[2]

Some of Milton's 'post-Eliot' critics were prepared to concede that he was, in some vague sort of way, a great poet, but this concession was usually attended by disabling qualifications. Many of these critics, for example, conveyed the impression that they felt uncomfortable at having to treat his work as *English* poetry. They tended to present him as a special case, a unique figure whose greatest poem was essentially a triumph—and in many ways an unfortunate triumph—over the English poetic tradition. To them, it seemed that Milton's stylistic achievements in *Paradise Lost* involved the sacrifice of the natural resources of his native language. In the Leavisite view, he thus forfeited 'all possibility of subtle or delicate life in his verse'.[3]

For a long time this conception of the epic style held its ground, in spite of the fact that it was not supported by really convincing evidence. The adverse critics seemed to take it for granted that the few passages they selected for censure could fairly be regarded as typical of the whole poem. This, however, was an unfounded assumption; the style of *Paradise Lost* is remarkable, above all, for its variety, and to condemn the whole twelve books because half-a-dozen passages were found, on analysis, to be ritualistic in movement and deficient in subtlety and sensitivity was surely unjustified. Nevertheless, several Miltonists were prepared to accept the verdict that in *Paradise Lost* Milton's rhythms were non-organic and that the Grand Style did not exhibit any expressive closeness to the movements of actual sensory experience. Indeed, Bernard Bergonzi went so far as to suggest that 'Leavis has certainly established' that qualities like sensitivity, subtlety and expressive closeness to the senses are not present in Milton's verse.[4]

But to the great majority of Milton's apologists, it mattered little whether charges of sensuous poverty and non-organic rhythms were justified, because they held the view that such charges, whether justified or not, were irrelevant. C. S. Lewis spoke for such critics when he noted a peculiar difficulty in meeting the critics of the epic style: 'that they blame it for the very qualities which Milton and his lovers regard as virtues'.[5] Lewis and other defenders of Milton's Grand Style argued that the adverse critics failed to take account of genre and epic decorum, and that in seeking such qualities as closeness to the movements of actual sensory experience they were seeking, and generally not finding, qualities which would, in any case, be out of place in *Paradise Lost*, or which were not really essential to a successful epic poem. This defence of the epic style was based on the view that nothing could mean less than a contrast between the ritual style of *Paradise Lost* and the lyrical, conversational style of Donne or the dramatic style of Shakespeare. R. M. Adams has expressed the point of view of most of the defenders of the Grand Style. 'An epic style', he suggested, 'is narrative, didactic, rhetorical, continuously elevated, and directly exemplary; it cannot go very far in the direction of becoming colloquial or witty or social without ceasing to be epic. It cannot shift tone radically or modulate very far from its major key without throwing things off balance.'[6] Miltonists were, on the whole, quite content to rely on the argument that the style of *Paradise Lost* exemplified, to a remarkable degree, the qualities always associated with epic poetry, and that it was futile to criticize it for conforming so admirably to the laws of its relevant poetic genre.

There was a striking similarity between the methods employed by critics in defence of the style of *Paradise Lost* and those employed by defenders of its structure—especially against Waldock's criticisms. Pointing out that modern readers have acquired, through the novel in particular, kinds of literary experience that Milton lacked, Waldock went on to evaluate *Paradise Lost* in the light of this experience, and suggested that the epic, as a narrative poem, did not possess the coherence and psychological plausibility which modern readers tend to expect from narrative works. The commonest answer to Waldock's kind of criticism was that his remarks, while interesting, were really irrelevant to *Paradise Lost*. Bernard Bergonzi's reaction was fairly typical. Appealing to genre, he argued that 'behaviour in the novel is inevitably involved with a complex of assumptions relating to the existing order of society, and the conventions governing the form are all intensely naturalistic. Any concept of narrative that can be drawn from the novel must inevitably be affected by these conditions, and nothing could be more certain than that it would be wholly inapplicable to such a poem as *Paradise Lost*.'[7] Critics like Bergonzi were prepared to admit that Waldock's case was probably unanswerable within the terms of reference in which it was expressed; they insisted, however, that it was wrong in failing to take account of the wide differences between a seventeenth-century epic and a twentieth-century novel.

Milton's apologists pleaded continually that the reader should take into account the conventions of seventeenth-century thought, the conventions governing the style and diction of epic poetry, and the necessary differences between epic verse and lyrical and dramatic verse. Professor Wright, for example, criticized Waldock's assumption that we modern readers need take no account of 'differences in conventions of thought and feeling between the seventeenth century and our own'. Waldock's ideal readers, 'natural, easygoing, unprejudiced', will, Wright suggested, misread the poem by substituting their own prejudices for Milton's. C. S. Lewis felt that the proper way to read *Paradise Lost* was to see Milton's world as if we believed it, 'and then, while we still hold that position in our imagination, to see what sort of poem results'. Rajan made it clear in his Preface that 'most of the chapters in this book represent an attempt to see *Paradise Lost* through the eyes of Milton's contemporaries'. And Douglas Bush claimed that 'the more one knows of all thought and learning and literature, the richer one's understanding and enjoyment of Milton are'.[8] All the critics mentioned reached extremely favourable verdicts on Milton's poetry. The unhistorical and even anti-historical readings presented by most of the adverse critics resulted, on the other hand, in far less favourable verdicts.

It is worth while investigating the implications of the 'historical' defence of Milton. Apologists for *Paradise Lost* and its style are clearly justified in appealing to genre, in insisting on the differences between the style appropriate to epic and that appropriate to drama. They are also justified in insisting on a recognition of the differences between the beliefs and ideas of seventeenth-century readers and those of the 'natural, easygoing, unprejudiced' readers of modern fiction. The suggestion that modern readers of *Paradise Lost* ought to forget for the time being their own prejudices and to read the poem as an ideal seventeenth-century reader would was made by most of its defenders. G. A. Wilkes pointed out that the most familiar arguments of Milton's apologists 'tend to instruct us on the response we should cultivate at this juncture or that, in place of the response we naturally give'.[9] If we are prepared to accept historical criticism as possessing a final and complete validity, then most of the issues raised by modern critics tend to become relatively unimportant. There is no real answer to those who defend Milton by arguing that we cannot blame him for having written a heroic poem in the heroic manner, and who adopt the strongminded position that in *Paradise Lost* 'we have the heroic subject and the Grand Style, and if these do not accord with the modern sensibility, so much the worse for the modern sensibility'.[10]

But the fact is that many modern critics, among them some who have had a formative influence on modern critical thought, are not prepared to accept the complete validity of historical criticism; for them, at least, the historical defence of Milton cannot be fully convincing. To the historical defence of *Paradise Lost*, which was that of Williams, Lewis, Grierson, Bush, Tillyard, Wright and others, two kinds of objection might be made. Although it may be reasonable to insist on the differences between epic and drama, between the seventeenth-century reader and the modern reader, it seems clear that it is extremely difficult, if not impossible, for modern readers to read a poem like *Paradise Lost* without allowing their reading to be affected by the prejudices of the present. There is the further consideration—and an even more important one in the light of modern critical theory—that a completely 'historical' reading of the epic, the natural consequence of the approach advocated by its 'historical' apologists, has one rather undesirable feature: it involves trying to isolate *Paradise Lost* from any vital contact with the present. A defence of the poem in purely historical terms is likely to do little more for Milton than to confirm his present 'classic' status: it altogether leaves out of account any consideration of his impact on, or relevance to, life and literature in the present. To say this is not to suggest that the relevance of a dead writer for modern readers is an absolutely certain indication of the value of his work: the needs and demands of the immediate present, for one thing, may not be those of the future, a consideration which makes 'modern relevance' on its own an unstable and doubtful criterion. But a defence of Milton which could both suggest and demonstrate the 'living' quality of his work, and at the same time provide an 'historical' vindication, would seem to provide a more satisfactory basis for admiration than a purely 'academic' one.

In an essay on Ben Jonson, T. S. Eliot raised issues which are relevant to Milton. Eliot did not deny to Jonson the title of a great poet, but he suggested that Jonson's apologists had made him a safe academic classic and had failed to suggest why his poetry might be read with enjoyment. Eliot's diagnosis of the fate which overtook Jonson raises the question whether a similar—and hardly desirable—fate is likely to overtake Milton if he continues to be defended in predominantly 'historical' terms, and if his apologists fail to take account of modern tastes and conventions. Eliot wrote:

'The reputation of Jonson has been of the most deadly kind that can be compelled upon the memory of a great poet. To be universally accepted; to be damned by the praise that quenches all desire to read the book; to be afflicted by the imputation of the virtues which excite the least pleasure; and to be read only by historians and antiquaries—this is the most perfect conspiracy of approval. . . . No critic has succeeded in making him appear pleasurable or even interesting.'[11]

Eliot's words might well serve as a warning to Miltonists, far too many of whom have refused to come to terms, or to bring Milton to terms, with the contemporary situation.

Another remark of Eliot's about Jonson's reputation might be considered relevant to one aspect of the twentieth-century case against Milton: the charge that he had been a bad influence on later poets, and the suggestion that he was a poet whose work modern poets ought to avoid. In his attempt to explain the fate which had overtaken Jonson, Eliot suggested that 'Probably the fault lies with several generations of our poets. It is not that the value of poetry is only its value to living poets for their own work; but appreciation is akin to creation, and true enjoyment of poetry is related to the stirring of suggestion, the stimulus that a poet feels in his enjoyment of other poetry. Jonson has provided no creative stimulus for a very long time.'[12] This was clearly not intended as a charge against Jonson's poetry, but Eliot was able to suggest, as one of the causes of his decline, that poets had not found his influence a source of inspiration. Milton's influence on English poetry has waned steadily since Victorian times; we may well ask, in the light of Eliot's comments on Jonson, whether this can be the beginning of a gradual process of decline; whether, at some future time, Milton, like Jonson, will be read only by historians and antiquaries.

Milton's academic defenders were not, as a rule, prepared to take the arguments about his 'bad' influence really seriously. There is, however, a good deal to be said for the point of view represented in Eliot's remarks on Jonson. It is impossible not to feel that admirers of Milton would be in a happier position if influential modern poets found a creative stimulus in Milton's poetry. One important consequence of this—if these poets were also critics—would be living criticism, the lack of which Eliot deplored in the case of Jonson. Eliot pointed out that we have to go back to Dryden for a living criticism of Jonson's work. In direct contrast and opposition to the 'academic' defence of Milton by so many modern critics and scholars, we have Leavis's claim that a good critic endeavours, 'where the poetry of the past is concerned, to realize to the full the truism that its life is in the present or nowhere; it is alive in so far as it is alive for us'.[13] To the scholars and historians, on the other hand, the emphasis on creative stimulus and on the importance of poets of the past being 'alive' for the present meant little more than what Woodhouse called a 'new and usually concealed relativism'.[14]

In spite of the fact that the twentieth-century Milton Controversy often assumed the appearance of a battle between criticism and scholarship, it would be a mistake to divide the participants into two mutually exclusive categories, the critics who attacked and the scholars who defended. To do so would be to imply that the twentieth-century defence of Milton's work was conducted purely in scholarly and 'academic' terms. Not all of his apologists were content to see him as Eliot saw Jonson, 'damned by the praise that quenches all desire to read the book'. Some of them supplied at least some of the deficiencies implicit in scholarly approval by making a case for Milton's relevance to poets and readers of modern times. Those who find it difficult, or perhaps undesirable, to adopt an 'historical' approach may well follow the suggestion made by Professor Prince and read *Paradise Lost* in the light of Proust or Blake. And Professor Summers has given the discussion of Milton's ideas a decidedly 'modern' turn by pointing to the Lawrentian character of the treatment of human love in *Paradise Lost*.

There are reasons for supposing that Milton is unlikely to share the fate which overtook Ben Jonson. Eliot suggested that we have to go back to Dryden for a living criticism of Jonson; in Milton's case, on the other hand, living criticism continues to appear. The modern attack on Milton was part of the critical revolution associated with Pound and Eliot. But two other poets who played a leading part in that revolution—John Crowe Ransom and Allen Tate—have, as Cleanth Brooks pointed out, 'steadily, and from the beginning, put on record their admiration for Milton'.[15] A careful reading of *Four Quartets* serves to confirm the impression that in Eliot's second essay on Milton (1947), we have some excellent paragraphs of living criticism. Further evidence that Milton still continues to stimulate such criticism is to be found in a collection of essays—significantly titled *The Living Milton*—which appeared in 1960. The editor, Frank Kermode, described the ten contributors: 'Half of them are well-known poets. . . . I think it fair to say that all the contributors have found it possible to include Milton in a characteristically modern view of literature, to treat him as a living poet.'[16]

In any discussion of Milton's modern position, account must be taken of some important and far reaching developments in English literary criticism since the 'thirties. One such development—the emergence of 'verbal analysis' as the dominant critical method of our time—has caused misgivings among Miltonists. Many of them have expressed the view that Milton's work, especially *Paradise Lost*, does not respond satisfactorily to verbal criticism, or to what Professor Prince calls 'the search for implied ironies or ambiguities, for subtle correspondences between images and themes'.[17] Those who argue that the 'New Criticism' has little to contribute to our understanding of *Paradise Lost* generally give two reasons. Firstly, they argue, the techniques favoured by the 'New Critics' are appropriate only to short poems. Secondly, these techniques may have served admirably for symbolist and Metaphysical literature, for obscure and mystical works—the 'New Critics', indeed, found appropriate material in the works of writers like Yeats, Eliot and Joyce who employ language of symbols— but they are not at all appropriate to poetry such as Milton's, which is neither obscure nor symbolic.

The 'New Critics' have been accused of 'distorting the character' of Milton's poetry; their readings have been variously described as 'perverse and limited', as 'sheer imagination' and as, at best, 'secondary and supplemental'. They have also given the impression which may, on the whole, be a mistaken one, that they have had a rather low opinion of Milton. But in spite of the hostility which their methods have encountered from 'historical' critics and others (T. S. Eliot referred to verbal analysis as 'the lemon-squeezer school of criticism'), critics like William Empson, Cleanth Brooks and Christopher Ricks have contributed much to the elucidation of *Paradise Lost*, and have shown that verbal criticism is an interesting and profitable method of approaching the epic.[18]

Of all the modern objections to Milton's poetry, Leavis's attack on the whole Miltonic habit of language remains the most serious and the most fundamental. One difficulty in dealing with Leavis's objections to the style of *Paradise Lost* has already been stressed. It is that in his most important discussion of Milton's poetry—in *Revaluation*—he has condemned without offering any systematic defence of the grounds of his condemnation. He has made assumptions about poetry, unfavourable to Milton, without elaborating a theory in their defence. The nearest approach to a theory of poetry which adverse comment could elicit from Leavis was his reply to René Wellek's criticism of his *Revaluation*. Wellek asked him to defend his position 'abstractly and to become conscious that large ethical, philosophical and, of course, ultimately, also aesthetic *choices* are involved'.[19] Leavis, however, did not defend; he merely formulated what he had before implied. 'Poetry', he suggested, 'must be in serious relation to actuality, it must have a firm grasp of the actual, of the object, it must be in relation to life, it must not be cut off from direct vulgar living, it should be normally human. . . . Traditions, or prevailing conventions or habits, that tend to cut poetry in general off from direct vulgar living and the actual, or that make it difficult for the poet to bring into poetry his most serious interests as an adult living in his own time, have a devitalizing effect'.[20] Leavis did not associate these 'essential' qualities with Milton's poetry. But other critics, while they might agree that Leavis had described Milton's work accurately in his *Revaluation* chapter, would question his criteria and ask: Does he, in his answer to Wellek, express the whole story of 'good' poetry, and are his preferences to be regarded as absolutes? His opponents are surely justified in arguing that until it has been shown that Leavis's criteria are superior to all others, and the qualities he stresses are essential to poetry if we are to call it great, his rejection of the whole Miltonic habit of language is a matter of personal choice. But there is another aspect to the controversy originated by Leavis: some of the critics who agree with his view of what poetry should be also believe that Milton's poetry largely accords with that view. One of these critics, Christopher Ricks, sums up the situation neatly:

'The Milton controversy, then, is triangular. Leavis and Lewis agree as to what the poem *Paradise Lost* is, but differ as to what a poem should be, and so as to how good it is. Leavis and (say) Empson agree as to what a poem should be, but differ as to what the poem is, and so as to how good it is. Meanwhile Lewis and Empson agree as to how good the poem is, but differ about what it is and what a poem should be.'[21]

An attempt to sum up the Milton Controversy must be made at three different levels, because the controversy belongs partly to literary history, partly to literary criticism and partly to literary theory.

The arguments about Milton's influence and about his responsibility for the so-called 'dissociation of sensibility' belong to literary history. They now seem less important and less damaging to Milton than they did thirty years ago. This is largely due to the fact that the once influential concept of a seventeenth-century 'dissociation of sensibility', which provided a theoretical basis for a reading of literary history wholly unfavourable to Milton, has, during the past decade or so been almost completely discredited. In the 'twenties, Milton became the principal victim of a wholly new reading of literary history, a reading which occulted the tradition of which he was regarded as the chief representative, and which emphasized the hitherto largely neglected Metaphysical poets. This rewriting of English poetic history had a good deal to do with the aims and ambitions of T. S. Eliot. The history of English poetry was, to a certain extent, manipulated, even distorted, by Eliot and his followers in their search for precedents to vindicate the techniques of modern verse. Donne and the other Metaphysicals were made to seem almost contemporary, both in their use of language and in their ideas. But this reading of literary history has gradually become less acceptable, and the Donne vogue, which accompanied Milton's decline, has lost its momentum. The decline of Donne since 1930 could be illustrated in various ways. In *Revaluation* (1936), Leavis described him as 'contemporary—obviously a living poet in the most important sense'. By 1945, however, his position had altered considerably. Francis Scarfe, discussing the Apocalyptic Movement of the 'forties, wrote:

'I cannot see what Donne really has to do with it. Here is a prejudice unquestionably taken up from the Eliot generation. Donne, who under his clerical dress cleaned up a few of the scattered ends of the Renaissance, but who, far from being a liberator, reflects in his tortuous and painful style an ingrown nature; whose acceptance of the authority of Church and State suggests that today on a political plane he might have been a Fascist Laureate . . .'[22]

The portion of the Milton Controversy which belongs to literary criticism is more important, because the arguments of the literary critics, as distinct from those of the literary historians, have enjoyed a greater permanence, and continue to evoke lively debate. At the level of literary criticism, discussion must centre on this kind of question: What weaknesses in the verse and structure of the epic have been convincingly demonstrated? Even Milton's strongest admirers agree that there are places in *Paradise Lost* where the style and the treatment of the theme cannot be defended. As for the style, most people would agree with the suggestion of Ricks that 'there are moments when the language seems to be manipulated more from habit than from inner necessity'.[23] This is a serious charge, but its real force depends on the extent to which it is true of the poem as a whole: an important point at issue between critics and defenders of the epic style is the extent to which 'habit' predominates over 'inner necessity'. Flaws count, as John Peter pointed out, 'but how much they count depends less on their weight than their specific gravity, the ratio they bear to size, to mass and extent'.[24] *Paradise Lost*, as seen by the critics in the Leavisite tradition, is a poem in which grandeur and uniform elevation virtually exclude such qualities as subtlety and closeness to the movements of sensory experience. According to Leavis, it is also a poem which, after the first two books, 'though there are intervals of relief, becomes dull and empty'.[25] Even those who approve Leavis's criteria find such judgments arbitrary and extreme, unsupported as they are by any worthwhile analysis of the poem as a whole. In the view of most critics, they do not accord with the facts of the poem. For one thing, the virtual antithesis between grandeur and subtlety cannot be allowed; Ricks points out that these qualities often coexist in the very same lines:

> So glister'd the dire Snake, and into fraud
> Led Eve our credulous Mother, to the Tree
> Of prohibition, root of all our woe.
>
> IX. 643–645

And although we must agree with Dryden and Johnson that Milton has 'some flats among his elevations', the suggestion that ten books of the epic are mainly 'dull and empty' hardly deserves serious consideration.

No matter how far we pursue the arguments of the literary critics we shall be unlikely to arrive at a satisfactory conclusion: the Milton Controversy, like any other, involves a diversity of assumptions about literary value—assumptions which, as Wayne Shumaker points out, 'seem irrefutable precisely because they do not rest on evidence and therefore cannot be confuted by evidence'. The same writer describes admirably the kind of situation with which we are constantly faced when we try to decide on the merits of rival critical judgments of *Paradise Lost*:

'The man who believes it unarguable that literature should do so-and-so is likely, in disputation, to devote his energy to the demonstration that a poem or novel meets unspecified conditions, with the result that his failure to convince opponents who assume different conditions leaves him perplexed and doubtful of human sanity.' [26]

When all is said and done, the literary critics, while they can illuminate single aspects of the poem, can offer us little real help in our efforts to reach a final verdict on the merits of *Paradise Lost*. Ultimately, our view of Milton and his epic will roughly correspond to our philosophy and our theology, even to our politics. When we have read all that the critics have had to say about the Grand Style, we must still decide for ourselves whether we approve or condemn such 'un-English' lines as the following:

His journies end and our beginning woe.

III. 633

Our judgment of *Paradise Lost* may also depend on the extent to which we share the modern preference for the organic in art, for works in which form and content are almost, if not completely, fused. Milton's poem is used to illustrate the other extreme: his critics point to his 'externality', to the formal, inflexible movement of the verse as evidence of his lack of what Wordsworth called 'organic sensibility'. The Milton Controversy has raised and clarified many issues, but when we try to decide whether his qualities represent virtues or vices—assuming of course that we can agree as to what these qualities actually are—we have, as Adams points out, 'to deal with a bewildering number of contexts, whereby the same quality which accords ideally with one set of premises may be seen as irrelevant or objectionable to another'. The same writer reached the rather dispiriting conclusion that 'anyone who is determined to admire or condemn Milton's verse can find in these varied contexts ample material for either purpose.'[27] This is, perhaps, the real lesson of the Milton Controversy.

References

CHAPTER ONE

1 R. D. Havens: *The Influence of Milton on English Poetry*, Cambridge, Mass., 1922, p. 71.
2 F. R. Leavis: *Revaluation*, 1936, p. 42. See also J. Middleton Murry: *The Problem of Style*, 1922, and Ezra Pound: *Literary Essays*, ed. T. S. Eliot, 1954.
3 T. S. Eliot: 'A Note on the Verse of John Milton', *ESEA*, 1936; Pound, op. cit., 1960 edn., p. 217.
4 Preface to Pound, op. cit., p. xi.
5 Ibid.
6 Letter to *TLS*, 19 September 1958.
7 D. Davie in *The Living Milton*, ed. F. Kermode, 1960, p. 83.
8 James Thorpe, ed. *Milton Criticism*, 1951, p. 18.
9 E. M. W. Tillyard: *The Miltonic Setting*, 1938, pp. 44 and 131.
10 F. R. Leavis: *The Common Pursuit*, 1962 edn., p. 43n.
11 George Watson: *The Literary Critics*, 1962, pp. 99–100.
12 Havens, op. cit., p. 31.
13 Watson, op. cit., p. 100.
14 W. Bagehot: *Literary Studies*, 1905, ii, p. 217.
15 W. Raleigh: *Milton*, 1900, p. 151.
16 B. A. Wright: *Milton's 'Paradise Lost'*, 1962, p. 9.
17 F. R. Leavis: *New Bearings in English Poetry*, 1950 edn., p. 221; *The Common Pursuit*, p. 32.

CHAPTER TWO

1 F. R. Leavis: *Revaluation*, 1936, p. 52.
2 Logan Pearsall Smith: *Milton and His Modern Critics*, 1941; Cleanth Brooks: 'Milton and Critical Re-Estimates', *PMLA*, Vol. LXVI, No. 6, p. 1046; James Thorpe: *Milton Criticism*, 1951, p. 18.
3 John Peter: 'Reflections on the Milton Controversy', *Scrutiny* XIX, October 1952, p. 5.
4 A. J. A. Waldock: *'Paradise Lost' and its Critics*, 1947, p. 139.
5 C. S. Lewis: *A Preface to 'Paradise Lost'*, 1942, p. 130.
6 B. Rajan: *'Paradise Lost' and the Seventeenth-Century Reader*, 1947, p. 112.
7 Peter, op. cit., p. 13.

8 J. H. Hanford: *A Milton Handbook*, New York, 1926; 4th edn., 1946, p. 310.
9 B. A. Wright: *Milton's 'Paradise Lost'*, 1962, pp. 64–5.
10 J. H. Summers: *The Muse's Method*, 1962, pp. 22–3.
11 F. R. Leavis, op. cit., pp. 44 and 54.
12 R. D. Havens: *The Influence of Milton on English Poetry*, pp. 56–7, 60.
13 F. R. Leavis, op. cit., p. 54.
14 Rajan, op. cit., p. 124.
15 R. M. Adams: *IKON: John Milton and the Modern Critics*, Cornell, Ithaca, 1955, p. 181.
16 F. R. Leavis, op. cit., pp. 53–4.
17 C. L. Wrenn: 'The Language of Milton', *Studies in English Language and Literature Presented to Professor Karl Brunner* (*Wiener Studien zur englischen Philologie*, LXV, 1957), pp. 264–5. See also Professor Wrenn's *The English Language*, 1949: revised 1952, pp. 170–5.
18 *The Spectator*, 26 January 1712.
19 See Ezra Pound: *Literary Essays*, ed. T. S. Eliot, 1960 edn., p. 238; J. Middleton Murry: *The Problem of Style*, Chapter V; T. S. Eliot: *On Poetry and Poets*, 1957, p. 154; F. R. Leavis: *Revaluation*, Chapter II.
20 F. R. Leavis: *The Common Pursuit*, 1962 edn., p. 42.
21 Wright, op. cit., p. 65; Lewis, op. cit., p. 45. See Robert Bridges: *Milton's Prosody*, rev. edn., 1921.
22 Helen Darbishire: 'Milton's Poetic Language', *ESEA*, 1957, p. 45. See also Oliver Elton: *The English Muse*, 1932. 'Plain familiar words, in their natural order', Elton suggests, 'form the bedrock of his style' (p. 242).
23 Wrenn, op. cit., pp. 254–5.
24 See *TLS*, 19 September 1958, p. 529.
25 Bernard Bergonzi: 'Criticism and the Milton Controversy', *The Living Milton*, ed. F. Kermode, 1960, p. 174.
26 Ibid., p. 175.
27 Ibid., p. 175.
28 Christopher Ricks: *Milton's Grand Style*, 1963, p. 33.
29 John Peter: *A Critique of 'Paradise Lost'*, 1960, p. 164.
30 Ricks, op. cit., p. 9. See F. T. Prince: *The Italian Element in Milton's Verse*, Oxford, 1954. According to Professor Prince, Milton's Grand Style fulfilled the ideal of Tasso and his predecessors. Their demand was for a style which required continuous alertness on the part of the reader, not for one which allowed music to thrive at the expense of precise meaning. See also Summers, op. cit., who suggests that if we are to read *Paradise Lost*, 'we must not rule out the possibility that the poet may be more sensitive and more subtle, intellectually, morally and sensuously, than were we ourselves before we began to read his

poem'. Many of Milton's critics, however, feel able to approach
the poem without the slightest trace of diffidence.

31 William Empson: 'Milton and Bentley' in *Some Versions of Pastoral*,
1935, p. 157. John Crowe Ransom doubted Empson's interpretation, but in defence of Empson see Ricks, op. cit., pp. 105–6.

32 For Eliot's objection see *PBA*, 1947, XXXIII, p. 76n. Eliot's lecture
is reprinted in full in James Thorpe's *Milton Criticism*, but not in
Eliot's *On Poetry and Poets*. For Leavis's comment on the same
passage see *The Common Pursuit*, 1962 edn., p. 19n. For an answer
to these objections see Ricks, op. cit., pp. 11–13.

33 Ricks, op. cit., p. 75.

CHAPTER THREE

1 Frank Kermode: *Romantic Image*, 1957, p. 165.
2 F. W. Bateson: 'Contributions to a Dictionary of Critical Terms.
II. Dissociation of Sensibility', *Essays in Criticism*, July 1951,
p. 303.
3 T. S. Eliot: *Selected Essays*, 3rd edn., 1951, p. 287.
4 Ibid.
5 T. S. Eliot: *On Poetry and Poets*, 1957, pp. 143–4.
6 T. S. Eliot: *Selected Essays*, p. 303.
7 Herbert Read: *Collected Essays in Literary Criticism*, 2nd edn.,
1951, p. 287.
8 Donald Bush: *Paradise Lost in Our Time*, New York, 1945, p. 9.
9 George Williamson: *The Donne Tradition*, 1961 edn., p. 160.
10 F. R. Leavis: *Revaluation*, 1936, p. 71.
11 Herbert Read: *Collected Essays*, p. 77.
12 F. R. Leavis: *Revaluation*, p. 71.
13 In *From Donne to Marvell*, ed. Boris Ford (Pelican *Guide to English
Literature*), 1956, p. 68.
14 *Milton*, 1930, p. 355.
15 Basil Willey: *The Seventeenth-Century Background*, 1934, pp. 87–8.
16 Ibid., p. 42.
17 L. C. Knights: *Explorations*, 1946, p. 93.
18 Kermode, op. cit., p. 140.
19 F. R. Leavis: *Revaluation*, p. 34.
20 Ibid., p. 33.
21 V. de Sola Pinto: *The English Renaissance*, 1938 (2nd edn. 1951),
p. 107.
22 L. C. Knights, op. cit., p. 108.
23 Harold Wendell Smith: 'The Dissociation of Sensibility', *Scrutiny*,
XVIII, 1951–2, p. 187.
24 *Humanitas*, Autumn 1946; quoted by Bateson, op. cit., p. 311.
25 F. W. Bateson: *Essays in Criticism*, April 1952, p. 214. Bateson, in
his *English Poetry: A Critical Introduction*, 1950, seems to attach

much more significance to Eliot's doctrine than he does in his 1951-2 comments. See p. 157 of *English Poetry* where Bateson writes: 'But in *Paradise Lost, Paradise Regained* and *Samson Agonistes* the references to classical mythology are normally accompanied by a reminder that it is not *true*. In many passages the reader is specifically warned that these things are "fables" or "fabled". . . . These notice-boards, as they might be called ("Warning. This way to beauty. Go back for Truth"), are an indication of the arrival of Eliot's "dissociation of sensibility".'

26 *Essays in Criticism*, July 1951, p. 304. Bateson in his analysis shows quite clearly that *emotion* does not come into Eliot's theory at all: 'feeling' means 'sensation', not 'emotion'. From this it follows that many of the scholars and critics who provided glosses of 'dissociation of sensibility' did not understand exactly what Eliot was suggesting. Professor Willey, for example, equates 'feeling' with 'emotion' in one of his glosses in *The Seventeenth-Century Background*, p. 87. The following sentence from Professor Knight's essay on Bacon seems to indicate that he too believed that 'emotion' had some part in Eliot's doctrine: 'But the whole trend of Bacon's work is to encourage the relegation of instinctive and emotional life to a sphere separate from and inferior to the sphere of "thought" and practical activity' (*Explorations*, p. 108). There are numerous other examples.

27 *Essays in Criticism*, July 1951, p. 304.

28 Ibid., April 1952, pp. 207-13.

29 Ibid., p. 210.

30 J. B. Leishman: *The Monarch of Wit*, 1955, pp. 98-9.

31 See Rosemond Tuve: *Elizabethan and Metaphysical Imagery*, 1947.

32 *The Monarch of Wit*, p. 92. Tillyard writes: 'I do not mean to deny Donne's successes, but their relative frequency is less than those who know him chiefly from Professor Grierson's *Metaphysical Poetry* are aware' (*Milton*, p. 358).

33 J. B. Leishman, op. cit., p. 133.

34 T. S. Eliot: *Selected Essays*, pp. 138-9.

35 In *A Garland for John Donne*, ed. Theodore Spencer, Harvard, 1931, p. 8.

36 In the light of his comments on Donne and Chapman in 1927 and 1931, Eliot's belief, expressed in 'Milton II', 1947, that his theory retained 'some validity' is not easy to understand.

37 *Scrutiny*, XVIII, 1951-2, p. 179.

38 R. M. Adams: *IKON: John Milton and the Modern Critics*, 1955, p. 208.

39 In *From Dryden to Johnson*, ed. Boris Ford, 1956, pp. 61-2.

40 Kermode attacked Eliot's doctrine in *Romantic Image*, 1957; in an article, 'Dissociation of Sensibility', *The Kenyon Review*, XIX, Spring 1957; and in 'A Myth of Catastrophe', *Listener*, 8 and 15 November 1956.

41 Frank Kermode: *Romantic Image*, p. 143. J. B. Broadbent (*Some Graver Subject*, 1960, p. 206) sees Eliot's theory in much the same terms. 'Owing to the nature of sensibility', he suggests, 'to postulate its dissociation in the past can only be to relate an aetiological myth, for our view of it must be ethnocentrically distorted by our own and by our movement away from both even as we construct the theory.'

42 Kermode, op. cit., p. 145.

43 Ibid., p. 141.

44 Eliot: *Essays in Criticism*, July 1951, p. 309.

45 Kermode, op. cit., p. 145.

CHAPTER FOUR

1 F. R. Leavis: *The Common Pursuit*, 1962 edn.

2 G. Williamson: *The Donne Tradition*, Cambridge, Mass., 1930, p. 57.

3 Northrop Frye: *Anatomy of Criticism*, Princeton, 1957, p. 18.

4 J. H. B. Masterman: *The Age of Milton*, 1897, p. 6.

5 H. Sykes Davies, ed.: *The Poets and their Critics*, Vol. I, 2nd edn., 1960, p. 85.

6 Walter Raleigh: *Milton*, pp. 183–4 and 256.

7 Ibid., pp. 256 and 264.

8 F. R. Leavis: *The Common Pursuit*, 1962 edn., p. 36.

9 T. S. Eliot: *Selected Essays*, 3rd edn., 1951, p. 290.

10 George Watson: *The Literary Critics*, 1962, p. 189.

11 F. R. Leavis: *The Common Pursuit*, p. 292.

12 E. M. W. Tillyard: *Milton*, 1930, p. 368.

13 F. R. Leavis: *Revaluation*, pp. 28–9. The exclusion of Milton from various 'significant' traditions of English poetry has its parallel in Leavis's exclusion of Dickens from the Great Tradition of the English Novel.

14 Williamson: *The Donne Tradition*, p. ix.

15 Ibid., pp. 241, 160, and 32.

16 Herbert Read: *Collected Essays in Literary Criticism*, 1938; 2nd edn., 1951, p. 83.

17 Ibid., p. 45.

18 Gilbert Phelps: *A Short History of English Literature*, 1962, p. 25.

19 F. W. Bateson: *English Poetry: A Critical Introduction*, 1950, p. 255. Leavis's extension of the seventeenth-century tradition of wit to include Pope involved some of his disciples in research aimed at establishing Pope's affinities with the Metaphysicals and Jonson. Geoffrey Walton concluded that Pope 'inherited a large share of Metaphysical wit coming from Donne, but a predominant aspect of his genius, the Augustan decorum, can be traced back to Donne's contemporary, Jonson'. (*Metaphysical to Augustan*, 1955, p. 23.)

20 F. R. Leavis: *New Bearings in English Poetry*, 1950 edn., p. 82

Convincing evidence of the success achieved by Leavis's reading of literary history can be found in the various volumes of the Pelican *Guide to English Literature*. The volume dealing with the period 1603–1660 is entitled, significantly, *From Donne to Marvell*. The whole account of Milton's style written by R. G. Cox reads like a summary of the relevant chapter in *Revaluation*. Donne is mentioned far more often than Milton, and headings like 'Poetry and the Tradition of Wit' and 'Later Developments of Wit in Poetry' show the affinity of this work with Leavis's critical ideas.

21 F. R. Leavis: *New Bearings*, p. 9.
22 T. S. Eliot: *Selected Essays*, 1951 edn., p. 290.
23 F. R. Leavis: *The Common Pursuit*, p. 280.
24 See his lecture, 'The Frontiers of Criticism', reprinted in *On Poetry and Poets*, 1957.
25 T. S. Eliot: *On Poetry and Poets*, p. 106.
26 J. B. Leishman: *The Monarch of Wit*, p. 90.
27 T. S. Eliot: *On Poetry and Poets*, p. 159.
28 A. S. P. Woodhouse: 'The Historical Criticism of Milton', *PMLA*, Vol. LXVI, p. 1043.
29 T. S. Eliot in *A Garland for John Donne*, 1931, p. 8.
30 John Holloway: in *The Modern Age*, ed. B. Ford; 2nd edn., 1963, pp. 97–8.
31 See her essay, 'Four Quartets: A Commentary', in *T. S. Eliot: A Study of his Writings by Several Hands*, ed. B. Rajan, 1948, pp. 74–5.
32 J. B. Leishman: *The Monarch of Wit*, p. 91.

CHAPTER FIVE

1 Ezra Pound: *Literary Essays*, ed. T. S. Eliot, 1960, p. 238.
2 J. Middleton Murry: *Studies in Keats New and Old*, 2nd edn., 1939, p. 110.
3 *Oxford Book of Christian Verse*, 1940, p. xvii.
4 Logan Pearsall Smith: *Milton and His Modern Critics*, 1940, p. 32.
5 Ibid., p. 49.
6 T. S. Eliot: *On Poetry and Poets*, 1957, p. 141.
7 F. R. Leavis: *The Common Pursuit*, 1962 reprint, p. 23.
8 T. S. Eliot: *Selected Essays*, 3rd edn., 1951, p. 319.
9 Quoted in Thorpe: *Milton Criticism*, 1951, p. 253.
10 B. Bergonzi: in *The Living Milton*, ed. F. Kermode, 1960, p. 178.
11 William Empson: *Milton's God*, 2nd edn., 1965, p. 25.
12 Logan Pearsall Smith: *Milton and His Modern Critics*, pp. 49–50.
13 Douglas Bush: *Paradise Lost in Our Time*, New York, 1945, p. 27.
14 T. S. Eliot: *On Poetry and Poets*, p. 148.
15 Charles Williams, ed.: *The English Poems of John Milton*, 1940, Introduction, p. viii.
16 Denis Saurat: *Milton Man and Thinker*, 1946 edn., p. xi.

17 William Riley Parker: *Milton's Contemporary Reputation*, Ohio State University Press, 1940, p. 52.

18 *v.* Newman's essay, 'English Catholic Literature'; Letters of Hopkins to Bridges, ed. C. C. Abbott, 1935; Hilaire Belloc: *Milton*, 1935; E. H. Visiak: *The Portent of Milton*, 1958, p. 54.

19 Helen Darbishire, ed.: *Early Lives of Milton*, 1932, pp. vii–x.

20 Ibid., p. xxvii.

21 Helen Darbishire attributes the anonymous biography to Milton's nephew, John Phillips, basing her attribution on the evidence of handwriting and of some characteristic spellings in the text. However the first editor of the anonymous biography, Edward S. Parsons, suggests Dr Paget, Milton's physician. See the article by Parsons, 'Concerning *The Earliest Life of Milton*', *ELH*, IX, 1942, pp. 106–17. The anonymous biography is, as Parsons points out, the one seventeenth-century biography in which Milton 'is treated with entire sympathy'. If Miss Darbishire's choice of John Phillips is correct, she has made a strong point in Milton's favour. John Phillips, as she points out, 'was the scapegrace nephew who got into trouble with the Council over a licentious book of songs, wrote a coarse *Satyr* upon the Presbyterians that was to enjoy a prolonged popularity with the Royalists, and as far as we can see had nothing at all of the Puritan in his composition'. (Darbishire, op. cit., p. xxxi.)

22 Helen Darbishire, op. cit., p. xl.

23 B. A. Wright: *Milton's 'Paradise Lost'*, 1962, p. 9.

24 Jonathan Richardson, father and son: *Explanatory Notes and Remarks on Milton's Paradise Lost . . . with a Life of the Author . . . by Jonathan Richardson senior*, 1734.

25 Charles Williams: 'The New Milton', *The London Mercury*, July 1937, p. 257.

26 Masson: *Life of Milton*, 1859–80, vol. III, p. 46.

27 *v.* Darbishire, op. cit., p. xl.; Burns Martin: 'The Date of Milton's First Marriage', *SP*, xxv, 1928, pp. 457–62; B. A. Wright: 'Milton's First Marriage', *MLR*, xxvi, 1931, pp. 383–400, and xxvii, 1932, pp. 6–23. Tillyard, in his *Milton*, 1930, was not completely convinced by Martin's alteration of the traditional dating to 1642. 'I do not think', Tillyard wrote, 'we are justified in doubting Phillips. Being Milton's pupil at the time, he was certain to have observed and remembered the domestic happenings' (*Milton*, p. 140). Wright's arguments for 1642, however, appear conclusive.

28 The principal contributions to the discussion of Milton's possible 'forgery', apart from those of Liljegren, Morand, and Empson are: John S. Smart: 'Milton and the King's Prayer', *RES*, I, 1925, pp. 385–91; R. W. Chambers: 'Poets and their Critics: Langland and Milton', *PBA*, xxvii, 1941, pp. 144–54; F. F. Madan: *New*

Bibliography of the Eikon, 1950. Those who have discussed the question are pretty evenly divided: Liljegren, Morand and Empson accepted the story that Milton was responsible for the forgery—with varying degrees of conviction. Smart, Chambers and Madan rejected it completely. Tillyard was not sure. (*v. Milton*, p. 187.) Neither was Grierson. (*v. The Year's Work in English Studies*, 1920–1, p. 104.) Hanford (*A Milton Handbook*, p. 108), considered the arguments of Smart decisive against the story. Saurat, on the other hand, saw no good reason for rejecting it. (*v. RES*, III, 1927, p. 355.) Empson makes an important point when he says that it is no use for Milton's defenders to protest that nobody heard of the forgery until forty years after it was supposed to have taken place: he points out that the Royalist publishers already suspected the forgery in 1650 (*Milton's God*, p. 290).

29 William Empson: *Milton's God*, p. 318.

30 Darbishire, op. cit., p. xlix.

31 Here is Johnson's version of the story of Milton's service to Davenant; he is referring to Milton's escape from punishment after the Restoration: 'A very particular story of his escape is told by Richardson in his *Memoirs*, which he received from Pope, as delivered by Betterton, who might have heard it from Davenant. In the war between the King and Parliament, Davenant was made prisoner and condemned to die; but was spared at the request of Milton. When the turn of success brought Milton into like danger, Davenant repaid the benefit by appearing in his favour'. (*Life of Milton*.) There is, however, more evidence in favour of the story than Johnson gives here. Apart from the anonymous biographer, whose work Johnson did not know, Richardson's account is corroborated by two other witnesses, Anthony Wood, in his *Life of Davenant*, and Jacob Tonson in a letter. (See Darbishire, op. cit., Introduction and p. 30, and B. A. Wright: *Milton's 'Paradise Lost'*, p. 28.)

32 J. Milton French: 'The Powell-Milton Bond', *Harvard Studies and Notes*, XX, 1938, p. 73.

33 E. H. Visiak: *The Portent of Milton*, p. 89. Also Douglas Bush: *English Literature in the Earlier Seventeenth Century*, 1945, p. 370.

34 Keats: Letter of 3 May 1818; Shelley: *A Defence of Poetry*, 1821; Leigh Hunt: *Imagination and Fancy*, 1844; Bagehot's review of Masson's *Life of Milton*, reprinted in *Literary Studies*, I, ed. R. H. Hutton, 1859. See James Thorpe: *Milton Criticism*, pp. 8–15.

35 Walter Raleigh: *Milton*, p. 88.

36 A. J. A. Waldock: *'Paradise Lost' and its Critics*, p. 8.

37 F. R. Leavis: *Revaluation*, p. 53.

38 J. H. Hanford: *SP*, XVI, 1919, p. 141.

39 E. Greenlaw: 'A Better Teacher than Aquinas', *SP*, XIV, 1917, p. 201.

40 See Liljegren: *Studies in Milton*, Lund, 1919. Liljegren tried to show that Milton had lied in *Areopagitica* about his visit to Galileo, 'in order to obtain public employment and rise in the state', because 'if any man could claim attention from the Parliament, it would be he who among his acquaintances counted Galileo, the most famous man of the century'. (Liljegren, p. 36.) See also L. I. Bredvold: 'Milton and Bodin's *Heptaplomeres*', *SP*, XXI, 1924, pp. 399–407. Bredvold discovered that Milton possessed a copy of *Colloquium Heptaplomeres de abditis rerum sublimium arcanis.* This work, available only in manuscript in Milton's day—it was not printed until 1841—was full of [daring speculation, and extremely difficult to obtain. That Milton possessed a copy shows, as Tillyard puts it, 'how well acquainted with the most advanced thought of his time he must have been'. (*Milton*, p. 218.)

There is a good discussion of the work of the 'New Movement' in Saurat: '*La Conception Nouvelle de Milton*', *Revue Germanique*, XIV, 1923, pp. 113–141.

41 Denis Saurat: *Milton Man and Thinker*, 1946 edn., p. 238.

42 Basil Willey: *The Seventeenth-Century Background*, 1934, p. 247. Willey's chapter, 'The Heroic Poem in a Scientific Age', provides a convincing answer to those who think Milton incapable of precise, sustained or analytic thinking.

43 Commenting on the line describing the Atonement, 'Man stole the fruit, but I must climb the tree', Empson wrote: 'He climbs the tree to repay what was stolen, as if he was putting the apple back; but the phrase in itself implies rather that he is doing the stealing, that so far from sinless he is Prometheus and the criminal' (*Seven Types of Ambiguity*, 3rd edn., 1961, p. 232). Eliot described this reading as 'ludicrous'.

44 Raleigh, op. cit., p. 88.

45 B. Rajan: '*Paradise Lost*' *and the Seventeenth-Century Reader*, 1947, p. 35.

46 Maurice Kelley: *This Great Argument: A Study of Milton's De Doctrina as a gloss upon 'Paradise Lost'*, Princeton, 1941, p. 212.

47 Harris Fletcher: 'Milton and Yosippon', *SP*, XXI, 1924, p. 497. See also Fletcher: *Milton's Rabbinical Readings*, Urbana, Illinois, 1931; and E. C. Baldwin: 'Some Extra-Biblical Semitic Influences on Milton's Story of the Fall of Man', *JEGP*, XXVII, 1929, pp. 366–401.

48 Kelley, op. cit., p. 217. Kelley argues that Saurat's attempt to identify Milton's God with the Absolute of nineteenth-century philosophy was misguided. According to the post-Kantian concept, the Absolute is 'non-manifested' and cannot create, 'does not act', and from it 'nothing can proceed'. Milton, however, as Kelley shows (op. cit., p. 23), places no such limitations on his Deity.

49 Rajan, op. cit., p. 23.
50 Rajan, op. cit., p. 25. See Arthur Sewell: 'Milton's *De Doctrina Christiana*', *ESEA*, XIX, 1933, pp. 52–3. Also Tillyard: 'Milton and Protestantism', *The Miltonic Setting*, 1938.
51 C. S. Lewis: *A Preface to 'Paradise Lost'*, 1942, pp. 81 and 91. Not everybody accepts Lewis's verdict on the 'catholic' quality of the poem. See, for example, Malcolm Mackenzie Ross: *Poetry and Dogma*, Rutgers U.P., 1954, where it is argued that *Paradise Lost* is 'anthropocentric', not 'Christocentric'. See, however, an essay by Sister Miriam Joseph in *Laval Theologique et Philosophique*, VIII, 1952, pp. 243–84. In this essay, which she calls 'Orthodoxy in *Paradise Lost*', she finds the poem quite orthodox on the Trinity, and argues that an intelligent Catholic reader can enjoy it without fear of doctrinal offence. See also J. B. Broadbent: *Some Graver Subject*, 1960, p. 290. He stresses 'the explicit and for all essentials orthodox Theism which the poem's sequentia are founded on'. There is a useful discussion of the whole subject of orthodoxy in *Paradise Lost* in H. F. Robins: *If This be Heresy: A Study of Milton and Origen* Urbana, Illinois, 1963.

CHAPTER SIX

1 W. Empson: *Milton's God*, revised edn., 1965, p. 25. In dealing with Milton's God, Empson sometimes becomes involved in contradictions. 'But it seems to me', he writes on p. 25, 'that C. S. Lewis was also right when he protested that this the God of *Paradise Lost* is merely the traditional Christian God.' On p. 272, however, writing about God's intention 'to turn himself into the Absolute', he believes that 'Here Milton's God is morally very much better than the traditional God of Christianity, not worse as has so often been said in recent times.'
2 J. B. Broadbent: *Some Graver Subject*, 1960, p. 290.
3 Empson, op. cit., p. 260.
4 R. M. Adams: *IKON*, 1955, p. 205.
5 C. Day Lewis: *The Poetic Image*, 1965 edn., pp. 108–9; *From Blake to Byron*, ed. Boris Ford, 1961, p. 116; George Watson: *The Literary Critics*, 1962, p. 101.
6 John Wain: in *The Living Milton*, 1960, pp. 7–10.
7 Walter Raleigh: *Milton*, p. 84.
8 For a comment on this see Kenneth Muir: *John Milton*, 1955, p. 129.
9 F. T. Prince: 'On the Last Two Books of *Paradise Lost*', *Essays and Studies*, 1958, p. 49.
John Wain: *The Living Milton*, p. 180.
11 J. H. Summers: *The Muse's Method*, 1962, p. 88. See also a very interesting discussion of the same topic in 'Milton Regained', *TLS*, 15 February 1963.

REFERENCES

12 Bush: '*Paradise Lost*' *in Our Time*, 1957 edn., p. 57.
13 Tillyard: *The Miltonic Setting*, 1938, pp. 52–3.
14 John Wain: in *The Living Milton*, p. 10.
15 L. A. Cormican: 'Milton's Religious Verse' in *From Donne to Marvell*, ed. B. Ford, 1955, p. 176.
16 T. S. Eliot: *The Sacred Wood*, 1960 reprint, p. 160.
17 T. S. Eliot: *Selected Essays*, 3rd edn., 1951, pp. 136–7.
18 Prince, op. cit., p. 41.
19 F. Kermode: in *The Living Milton*, p. 86.
20 D. Bush: '*Paradise Lost*' *in Our Time*, p. 110.

CHAPTER SEVEN

1 A. J. A. Waldock: '*Paradise Lost*' *and its Critics*, 1947, p. 143.
2 F. R. Leavis: *The Common Pursuit*, 1962 edn., pp. 26–7.
3 J. Peter: *A Critique of* '*Paradise Lost*', 1960, p. ix.
4 B. Bergonzi: in *The Living Milton*, p. 170.
5 E. M. W. Tillyard: *Studies in Milton*, 1951, pp. 8–51; B. A. Wright: *Milton's* '*Paradise Lost*', 1962, Chapter 9. For Kermode's discussion see *The Living Milton*, p. 85 ff.
6 Joseph Addison: *The Spectator*, 3 May 1712.
7 Waldock, op. cit., pp. 51–2, 54–5. Dealing with Waldock's conclusion that Adam's Fall is due entirely to his love for Eve, John Peter writes: 'This is one of those critical *aperçus* which has the absoluteness that a fact has, and can never be undermined' (op. cit., p. 130).
8 Waldock, op. cit., p. 49.
9 Ibid., p. 56.
10 Ibid., pp. 73–4 and 77.
11 Ibid., pp. 77–8. An interesting discussion of Satan's role in *Paradise Lost* is to be found in Helen Gardner's essay, 'Milton's Satan and the Theme of Damnation in Elizabethan Tragedy', *English Studies*, 1948. Here she suggests that 'the figure of Satan, originally conceived dramatically, is developed dramatically throughout', and that Milton 'expended his creative energies and his full imaginative power in exploring the fact of perversity within a single heroic figure'. She goes on to make the suggestion that 'in this, as in much else, he is what we loosely call an Elizabethan, sacrificing simplicity of effect and strength of design to imaginative opportunity; creating the last great tragic figure in our literature and destroying the unity of the poem in doing so' (p. 65).
12 Waldock, op. cit., pp. 98–9; Peter, op. cit., p. 17.
13 Waldock, p. 101; Peter, p. 19.
14 *Literary Studies*, Everyman's Library edn., 1932, Vol. 1, pp. 165–6.
15 Raleigh, *Milton*, pp. 129, 132–3.

16 Waldock, pp. 26 and 18.
17 Peter, p. 160.
18 C. S. Lewis: *A Preface to 'Paradise Lost'*, p. 1.
19 Bergonzi: in *The Living Milton*, p. 178.
20 Ibid., p. 177.
21 Waldock, p. 55; Rajan: *'Paradise Lost' and the Seventeenth-Century Reader*, p. 72.
22 C. S. Lewis, op. cit., p. 65.
23 G. A. Wilkes: *The thesis of 'Paradise Lost'*, Melbourne, 1961, p. 28.
24 Ibid., p. 5.
25 Ibid., pp. 42 and 31.
26 John Peter: *A Critique of 'Paradise Lost'*, p. 96.
27 Ibid., pp. 126–7.
28 Quoted in L. C. Knights: *Explorations*, 1946, p. 15.
29 Walter Raleigh: *Milton*, 133.
30 C. S. Lewis, op. cit., p. 97.
31 L. C. Knights, op. cit., p. 10.
32 Waldock, p. 101; Peter, p. 19.
33 Wilkes, op. cit., p. 42.

CHAPTER EIGHT

1 George Watson: *The Literary Critics*, 1962, p. 122.
2 T. S. Eliot: *On Poetry and Poets*, 1957, p. 139.
3 Ibid., p. 145.
4 Alexander Pope: *Postscript to the Odyssey*, 1723; John Dennis: *The Grounds of Criticism in Poetry*, 1704; William Hazlitt: *On Shakespeare and Milton*, 1818; W. Raleigh: *Milton*, 1900, p. 180.
5 R. D. Havens: *The Influence of Milton on English Poetry*, 1922, p. 139.
6 T. S. Eliot, op. cit., p. 139.
7 F. R. Leavis: *Revaluation*, 1936, p. 11.
8 Ibid., p. 2.
9 J. Middleton Murry: *The Problem of Style* (1922), 1961 edn., p. 105.
10 F. R. Leavis: *The Common Pursuit*, 1962 edn., p. 42.
11 Bonamy Dobrée: 'Milton and Dryden: A Comparison and Contrast in Poetic Ideas and Poetic Method.' *ELH*, III, 1936, p.89.
12 H. J. C. Grierson: *Milton and Wordsworth*, 1937, p. 122.
13 Douglas Bush: *'Paradise Lost' in Our Time*, 1945 edn., p. 13.
14 Eliot, op. cit., p. 139.
15 Ibid., p. 152.
16 Ibid., p. 160.
17 Leavis, *The Common Pursuit*, p. 253.
18 Letter to Dixon, 5 October 1878; Letter to Bridges, 15 February 1879. From *The Letters of Gerard Manley Hopkins to Robert Bridges*, and *The Correspondence of Gerard Manley Hopkins and Richard Watson Dixon*, ed. C. C. Abbott, 1935.

REFERENCES

19 G. M. Hopkins: Letter to Dixon, 5 October 1878.
20 Donald Davie: *Purity of Diction in English Verse*, 1952, p. 164.
21 Ibid., p. 182.
22 T. J. B. Spencer: 'The Tyranny of Shakespeare', 1959 British Academy Lecture, reprinted in *Studies in Shakespeare*, 1964, ed. Peter Alexander. Reference to p. 158.
23 Basil Willey: *The Seventeenth-Century Background*, 1934, p. 206.

CHAPTER NINE

1 F. R. Leavis: *Revaluation*, p. 67.
2 J. Peter: 'Reflections on the Milton Controversy', *Scrutiny*, XIX, October 1952, p. 5.
3 Leavis, op. cit., p. 52.
4 Bernard Bergonzi: in *The Living Milton*, p. 174.
5 C. S. Lewis: *A Preface to 'Paradise Lost'*, p. 129.
6 R. M. Adams: *IKON*, p. 182.
7 *The Living Milton*, p. 177.
8 Douglas Bush: *'Paradise Lost' in Our Time*, p. 108.
9 G. A. Wilkes: *The Thesis of 'Paradise Lost'*, Melbourne, 1961, p. 2.
10 Adams, op. cit., p. 184.
11 T. S. Eliot: *The Sacred Wood*, 1960 edn., p. 104.
12 Ibid., p. 105.
13 Leavis: *Revaluation*, p. 2.
14 A. S. P. Woodhouse: 'The Historical Criticism of Milton', *PMLA*, LXVI, December 1951, p. 1043.
15 Ibid., p. 1046.
16 *The Living Milton*, ed. Frank Kermode, Introduction.
17 F. T. Prince: 'On the Last Two Books of *Paradise Lost*', *ESEA*, 1958, p. 47.
18 See particularly Empson's chapters on Milton in *Some Versions of Pastoral* and in *The Structure of Complex Words*; Cleanth Brooks: 'Milton and Critical Re-Estimates', *PMLA*, LXVI, 1951, and 'Milton and the New Criticism', *Sewanee Review*, 1951; C. Ricks: *Milton's Grand Style*, 1963.
19 F. R. Leavis: 'Literary Criticism and Philosophy', *The Common Pursuit*, 1962 edn., p. 211.
20 Ibid., p. 215.
21 Ricks, op. cit., p. 10.
22 F. Scarfe: *Auden and After*, 1945, p. 157.
23 Ricks, op. cit., p. 17.
24 John Peter: *A Critique of 'Paradise Lost'*, 1960, p. 166.
25 Leavis: *Revaluation*, p. 59.
26 Wayne Shumaker: *Elements of Critical Theory*, University of California Press, Berkeley and Los Angeles, 1964 edn., p. 82.
27 Adams, op. cit., p. 198.

Bibliography

The place of publication of books cited below is London, unless otherwise stated.

For Milton bibliographies see D. H. Stevens: *Reference Guide to Milton from 1800 to the Present Day* Chicago, 1930; supplement to 1957 by C. Huckaby, 1960. *Cambridge Bibliography of English Literature*, ed. F. W. Bateson, 4 vol. 1941, and the *Supplement*, ed. G. Watson 1957. There are useful bibliographies in D. Saurat's *Milton Man and Thinker* 1925 edn., New York; in J. H. Hanford's *A Milton Handbook* New York, 4th edn., 1946; in Douglas Bush: *English Literature in the Earlier Seventeenth Century* 1945; in E. M. W. Tillyard's essay on Milton, Writers and their Work: No. 26, revised 1964; and in Marjorie Hope Nicholson's *A Reader's Guide to John Milton* 1964. There is a good Milton bibliography in V. de Sola Pinto: *The English Renaissance, 1510–1688* revised edn., 1951.

Since the 'thirties, especially since T. S. Eliot expressed his dissatisfaction with Milton's personality and the Grand Style in 'A Note on the verse of John Milton' *ESEA*, XXI, 1935, most contributors to Milton studies have been either Miltonolaters or Miltonoclasts: very few have been able to deal significantly with his work without becoming involved in the controversy which followed Eliot's remarks. The case against Milton is well argued by F. R. Leavis in *The Common Pursuit* 1952, Chapters I and II, and in 'Idea and Image', *TLS*, 19 September 1958; also by John Peter: 'Reflections on the Milton Controversy', *Scrutiny* XIX, October 1952. Attempts to answer modern objections were made by the following: Logan Pearsall Smith: *Milton and his Modern Critics* 1940; Charles Williams: Introduction to *The English Poems of Milton* 1940; R. W. Chambers: 'Poets and their Critics: Milton and Langland', *PBA*, XXVII, 1941; Douglas Bush: *'Paradise Lost' In Our Time* New York, 1945 and 'Recent Criticism of Paradise Lost', *Philological Quarterly*, XXVIII, 1949; E. M. W. Tillyard: *The Metaphysicals and Milton* 1956. By far the most successful answer to modern criticisms of *Paradise Lost* is Bernard Bergonzi's chapter, 'Criticism and the Milton Controversy', in *The Living Milton*, ed. F. Kermode 1960.

More or less objective summaries of the main issues of the Milton Controversy can be found in the following: J. Thorpe: Introduction to *Milton Criticism: Selections from Four Centuries* 1951; Cleanth Brooks: 'Milton and Critical Re-estimates', *PMLA*, XLVI, No. 6 1951; L. D. Lerner: Introduction to *Milton: Poems*, Penguin, 1951 and R. M. Adams: *IKON: John Milton and the Modern Critics* Cornell, Ithaca, 1955.

Adverse criticism of the style of *Paradise Lost* is represented by: T. S. Eliot's two essays on Milton, reprinted in *On Poetry and Poets* 1957; F. R. Leavis: 'Milton's Verse', *Revaluation* 1936; Ezra Pound: 'The Renaissance' and 'Notes on Elizabethan Classicists', reprinted in *Literary Essays of Ezra Pound*, ed. T. S. Eliot 1954; L. C. Knights: 'Milton Again', *Scrutiny* XI, 1942; J. Peter: *A Critique of 'Paradise Lost'* 1960; D. Davie: *Articulate Energy* 1955 and 'Syntax and Music in *Paradise Lost*', *The Living Milton* 1960. The Grand Style is defended along traditional lines, mainly in terms of genre and epic decorum, by C. S. Lewis: *A Preface to 'Paradise Lost'* 1942; by E. M. W. Tillyard in *The Miltonic Setting* 1938; by Douglas Bush in the chapter on Milton in *English Literature in the Earlier Seventeenth Century* 1945 and by B. Rajan in *'Paradise Lost' and the Seventeenth-Century Reader* 1947. The 'New Critics' have been more lively and adventurous in their appreciation of Milton's epic style; for examples of their techniques see W. Empson: 'Milton and Bentley' in *Some Versions of Pastoral* 1935 and ' "All" in *Paradise Lost*' in *Structure of Complex Words* 1951; Cleanth Brooks: 'Milton and the New Criticism', *Sewanee Review* 1951, and C. Ricks: *Milton's Grand Style* 1963, perhaps the best modern treatment of the subject.

On Milton's language, C. L. Wrenn: 'The Language of Milton', *Studies in English Language and Literature Presented to Professor Karl Brunner*. Wiener Studien zur englischen Philologie, LXV, 1957, and Helen Darbishire: 'Milton's Poetic Language', *ESEA*, 1957, contain important remarks. Sir Walter Raleigh's *Milton* 1900 is extremely valuable on both style and language. On Milton's prosody see Robert Bridges: *Milton's Prosody* rev. edn., 1921 and S. E. Sprott: *Milton's Art of Prosody* 1953. On special aspects of the Grand Style see F. T. Prince: *The Italian Element in Milton's Verse* Oxford, 1954, a major study, and J. Whaler: 'The Miltonic Simile', *PMLA*, XLVI 1931. Other worthwhile studies are: Bonamy Dobrée: 'Milton and Dryden: A Comparison and Contrast in Poetic Ideas and

Poetic Method', *ELH*, III 1936; A. Stein: *Answerable Style* 1953, and L. A. Cormican: 'Milton's Religious Verse', *From Donne to Marvell*, ed. B. Ford 1956.

The best and most comprehensive treatment of Miltonic influence is R. D. Havens's monumental work, *The Influence of Milton on English Poetry* Cambridge, Mass., 1922, which deals with all the available English poetry written between 1660 and 1837. Milton's influence on Keats has been the subject of much modern discussion; the best study is that of W. J. Bate, *The Stylistic Development of Keats* 1945. In addition see: J. Middleton Murry: *The Problem of Style* 1922 and *Keats and Shakespeare* 1926; B. Ifor Evans: *Keats* 1934, and E. M. W. Tillyard: *The Miltonic Setting* 1938, Chapters II and VII. On Milton and modern poetry, the essays of Eliot and Pound, already referred to, contain some interesting comments. For general discussion of Milton's influence see F. R. Leavis: *New Bearings in English Poetry* 1932; new ed., 1950, and D. Davie: *Purity of Diction in English Verse* 1952.

On Milton's life, the principal authentic sources of biography have been collected by Helen Darbishire in *The Early Lives of Milton* 1932. See also J. M. French, ed., *The Life Records of John Milton*, 4 vols. New Brunswick, 1949–58. Useful studies are: J. H. Hanford: *A Milton Handbook* New York, 1925; 4th edn., 1946; E. M. W. Tillyard: *Milton* 1930; F. E. Hutchinson: *Milton and the English Mind* 1946. On particular episodes, especially Milton's first marriage and the *Eikon* forgery, the more important studies are mentioned in Chapter V and in the footnotes. For the *Eikon*, F. F. Madan: *A New Bibliography of the Eikon* Oxford *Bibliographical Society Publications*, London, 1950, is indispensable.

Milton's intellectual background has been the subject of intensive study. Many of the important contributions are mentioned or discussed by B. Rajan in *'Paradise Lost' and the Seventeenth-Century Reader* 1947. The following are particularly useful: E. E. Stoll: *Poets and Playwrights* Minnesota, 1930; Basil Willey: *The Seventeenth-Century Background* 1934; G. W. Whiting: *Milton's Literary Milieu* Chapel Hill, North Carolina, 1939; A. S. P. Woodhouse, ed.: *Puritanism and Liberty* 1938; P. P. Morand: *De Comus A Satan* Paris, 1939 and *The Effects of His Political Life upon John Milton* Paris, 1939; D. M. Wolfe: *Milton in the Puritan Revolution* New York, 1941; A. Barker: *Milton and the Puritan Dilemma* Toronto, 1942; G. N. Clark: *The Seventeenth*

Century 1929; rev. 1947; K. Svendsen: *Milton and Science* Harvard and Oxford, 1956; H. F. Fletcher: *The Intellectual Development of John Milton* Urbana, Illinois: Vol. I, 1956; Vol. II, 1963; For the work of Saurat, Greenlaw, Hanford, Liljegren and other writers of the 'New Movement' see Chapter Five. M. A. Larson: *The Modernity of Milton* Chicago, 1926 is also important.

There are several good accounts of Milton's theology. Maurice Kelley's study, *This Great Argument* Princeton, 1941, is generally accepted as a definitive account both of Milton's theology and of the doctrinal relationship between *Paradise Lost* and *De Doctriana Christiana*. Other studies include: A. Sewell: 'Milton's *De Doctrina Christiana*', *ESEA*, XIX, 1934 and *A Study of Milton's Christian Doctrine* 1939; H. J. C. Grierson: *Cross Currents in English Literature of the Seventeenth Century* 1929 and *Milton and Wordsworth: Poets and Prophets* 1937; H. F. Robins: *If This be Heresy: A Study of Milton and Origen* Urbana, Illinois, 1963. On Milton's debt to Talmudic writings see H. F. Fletcher: *Milton's Semitic Studies and Some Manifestations of Them in His Poetry* Chicago, 1926 and *Milton's Rabbinical Readings* Urbana, Illinois, 1931.

Studies of the literary and theological background to *Paradise Lost* and of other special aspects are: A. O. Lovejoy: 'Milton and the Paradox of the Fortunate Fall', *ELH*, IV, 1937; G. McColley: *Paradise Lost* 1940, a study of sources; C. M. Bowra: *From Virgil to Milton* 1945, in which *Paradise Lost* is examined in the light of the epic tradition; F. T. Prince: 'On the Last Two Books of *Paradise Lost*', *ESEA*, XI 1958, and I. G. MacCaffrey: *Paradise Lost as 'Myth'* Harvard and Oxford, 1959.

There are numerous good critiques of *Paradise Lost* as a narrative poem. Two notable attempts to show that there are serious weaknesses and inconsistencies in the narrative are those of A. J. A. Waldock: *'Paradise Lost' and Its Critics* 1947 and J. Peter: *A Critique of 'Paradise Lost'* 1960. The integrity of the poem is defended by G. A. Wilkes: *The Thesis of 'Paradise Lost'* Melbourne, 1961 and by A. D. Ferry: *Milton's Epic Verse: The Narrator in 'Paradise Lost'* 1963. Other studies of the evolution of Milton's narrative are: J. S. Diekhoff: *Milton's 'Paradise Lost': A Commentary on the Argument* 1946; E. M. W. Tillyard: 'The Crisis of *Paradise Lost*' in *Studies in Milton* 1951; J. B. Broadbent: *Some Graver Subject* 1960, and J. H. Summers: *The Muse's Method* 1962. On the characters of *Paradise Lost* see G. Rostrevor Hamilton: *Hero or Fool? A Study of Milton's Satan* 1944; Helen

Gardner: 'Milton's Satan and the Theme of Damnation in Elizabethan Tragedy', *ESEA* 1948; W. Empson: 'The Satan of Milton', *Hudson Review*, XIII 1960 and *Milton's God* 1961; rev. edn., 1965, as well as the works of Williams, C. S. Lewis, Waldock, Rajan, Peter and Wilkes, already mentioned. Allan H. Gilbert's *On the Composition of 'Paradise Lost'* Chapel Hill, North Carolina, 1947 is an interesting account of the manner in which Milton ordered his epic material.

For general studies of Milton's life and work see John Bailey: *Milton* 1915; K. Muir: *John Milton* 1955; D. Daiches: *Milton* 1957; B. A. Wright: *Milton's 'Paradise Lost'* 1962—a book in which modern critics are ably answered, and M. H. Nicholson: *A Reader's Guide to John Milton* 1964.

Index

Index

The principal topics discussed in the book are accurately described in the various chapter-headings; for this reason a subject index was not considered necessary.

INDEX

Milton, John (*cont.*)
55, 126; *De Doctrina Christiana*, 71, 83–6, 147, 155; *Defence of the English People*, 72; *Doctrine and Discipline of Divorce*, 74; *Eikonoklastes*, 75, 76; *In Quintum Novembris*, 77; *Lycidas* 126; *Nativity Ode*, 51, 117; *Of Reformation*, 76; *Paradise Regained*, 64, 142; *Samson Agonistes*, 64, 70, 117, 122, 123, 126, 142
Morand, Paul, 75, 145, 146, 154
Muir, Kenneth, 148, 156
Murry, J. Middleton, 1, 13, 15, 19, 23, 24, 66, 67, 68, 119, 139, 140, 144, 150, 154

Nashe, Thomas, 42, 45
'New Critics', 10, 28–30, 133, 153
Newman, Cardinal, 72, 145
Newton, Thomas, 10, 30, 85
Nicholson, M. H., 152, 156
Nott, Kathleen, 87

Origen, 148, 155
Owen, Wilfred, 57

Paget, Dr. (Milton's physician), 145
Parker, W. R., 71, 145
Parsons, E. S., 72, 145
Pater, Walter, 69
Pattison, Mark, 14
Peacock, T. L., 126
Pearce, Zachary, 29
Pemberton, Henry, 20
Pepys, Samuel, 71
Peter, John, 14, 16, 17, 28, 99, 100, 104–5, 107, 112, 114, 126, 136, 139, 140, 149, 150, 151, 152, 153, 155, 156
Phelps, Gilbert, 57, 143
Phillips, Edward (Milton's nephew), 9, 72, 73, 74
Phillips, John (Milton's nephew) 145
Pinto, V. de Sola, 40, 141, 152
Pius, V, Pope, 77

Pope, Alexander, 1, 3, 4, 5, 17–18, 37, 48, 50, 55, 57, 58, 116, 117, 118, 126, 143, 146, 150
Pound, Ezra, 1, 2, 3, 4, 11, 13, 14, 15, 19, 23, 24, 48–9, 57, 65, 66, 67, 68, 89, 95, 116, 120, 122, 126, 132, 139
Powell, Mary (Milton's first wife), 74
Powell, Richard (Milton's father-in-law), 76
Prince, F. T., 90–1, 132, 133, 140, 148, 149, 151, 153, 155
Proust, Marcel, 91, 92, 94, 132

Rajan, B., 16, 21, 80, 85, 86, 109, 129, 140, 144, 147, 148, 150, 153, 154, 156
Raleigh, Walter, 1, 4, 5, 8, 14, 22, 52, 53, 78, 79, 82–3, 84, 85, 86, 90, 96, 99, 105, 106, 110, 112, 113, 114, 115, 117, 118, 139, 143, 146, 147, 148, 149, 150, 153
Ransom, J. C., 132, 141
Read, Herbert, 2, 6, 11, 13, 34, 36, 39, 56, 141, 143
Richardson, Jonathan (senior), 9, 74, 146
Richardson, Jonathan, father and son, 10, 30, 145
Ricks, Christopher, 10, 28–30, 133, 134–5, 136, 140, 141, 151, 153
Robins, H. F., 148, 155
Ross, M. M., 148

Saintsbury, George, 14, 77
Salmasius, 72
Saurat, Denis, 66, 71, 77, 80–1, 82, 83, 84, 144, 146, 147, 152, 155
Scarfe, Francis, 135, 151
Schumaker, Wayne, 137, 151
Sewell, Arthur, 85, 148, 155
Shakespeare, 1, 11–12, 15, 21, 23, 28, 33, 37, 40, 50, 52, 57, 58, 94–6, 112, 113, 119, 120, 124, 126, 128, 150, 151, 154
Shelley, 34, 45, 56, 57, 77, 90, 105, 112, 146
Smart, J. S., 80, 145, 146